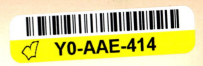

FIVE KIDNAPPED INDIANS

FIVE KIDNAPPED INDIANS

A True 17th Century Account
of Five Early Americans:

Tisquantum, Nahanada, Skitwarroes, Assocomoit and Maneday

by ANNE MOLLOY

illustrated by Robin Jacques

Hastings House, Publishers, New York

Published 1968
by Hastings House Publishers, Inc.

Originally titled *Captain Waymouth's Indians*
this edition includes a new bibliography, notes,
index and illustrations, and is published in collaboration
with Richard Sadler Ltd., Chalfont St. Giles, Buckinghamshire, England.

Library of Congress Catalog Card Number: 56 – 11304

Published simultaneously in Canada by Saunders of Toronto, Ltd.,
Don Mills, Ontario, Publishers, Toronto 2B

Printed and bound in Germany (East)

CALIBAN:

    "When thou camest first,
    Thou strok'st me, and made much of me; wouldst give me
    Water with berries in't; and teach me how
    To name the bigger light, and how the less,
    That burn by day, and night; and then I lov'd thee,
    And show'd thee all the qualities o' th' isle,
    The fresh springs, brine-pits, barren places and fertile;
    Curs'd be that I did so!"

The Tempest, ACT I, SCENE 2

INTRODUCTION

ALTHOUGH I GREW UP in New England where Indians had lived, as a child I never saw one.

A coin-silver tablespoon, worn thin at the tip and brought out only for special family occasions such as Thanksgiving Day, was my first introduction to the Indians of New England. This spoon had been buried with other valuables in an iron kettle during a time of Indian raids. Later, it was dug up when the settlers felt safe and handed down in the family until it came to us. It wasn't until I was considered old enough to listen to tales of savagery that I gained more knowledge of Indians. Among the tales my grandfather told me was one of a long-ago grandmother who had killed ten sleeping Indians in 1697 and wrapped their bloody scalps in a linen towel. My grandfather considered her actions quite justified; raiding Indians had burned her house to the ground, killed her new-born child before her eyes, and were carrying her into captivity in Canada. My grandfather remembered seeing the very towel she had used. How I wished that I might have.

Then for many years my sole contact with Indians was in learning to master the names which they had put upon our land. They make mighty difficult spelling. When you grow up in the state of Massachusetts, visit Lake Winnipesaukee, and study the convolutions of the Connecticut River on a schoolroom map, you do wonder about the men who gave us these spelling problems and why they are no longer about.

I was quite grown up when I saw my first Indians face to face. They had come into a Maine town to shop after a week of raking wild blueberries and had eyes only for what was in the store windows. They would have been surprised to know how the sight of them set my heart to beating with excitement. They were dressed like anyone else, although more poorly than many. To my surprise they were not red skinned nor even copper-coloured as they are in the stories. Rather, they looked merely suntanned. Their voices, speaking a language I did not know, were gentle. They were short with delicate hands and small feet. How different from the murdering devils of the tales.

Suddenly I wanted to know what sort of people the New England Indians really were when the first Europeans came to these shores. Was there perhaps a different sort of people before the settlers met with such cruel savagery?

I went to the libraries to find an answer in the first-hand accounts written by early arrivals on the New England shore. It was in this way that I first met the five Indians who were kidnapped by Captain Waymouth. In my fascination with their story I became a library detective. I looked for clues as to what happened next to each one of the five. I searched for witnesses who had reported meeting one or another of them in their wanderings. Whenever a dull brown, dust-covered book contained a sentence or two that filled in a blank, my heart beat even faster than on the day when I first met a live Indian. And to my surprise and delight there were many who had troubled to write down what small bit they knew about the five kidnapped ones.

ANNE MOLLOY

FOREWORD

THESE ARE THE STORIES of five Indians who were kidnapped on the coast of Maine in the year 1605 and carried to England.

The tales are all true. They were written down by seafaring men, explorers, and colonists of those times. Never are the Indians the heroes of the accounts. They were hardly considered human beings by those who wrote about them, and their stories have to be picked out, a bit from one man's tale, a piece from another's. And it is only when one of the five savages

is being useful to his captors that he appears in the
records at all! Sometimes we wonder that the Indians
are even mentioned, what with their lack of importance to the white man and the difficulty of writing down for the first time the words and names of a
strange tongue.

One of these five Indians is well known to us
as Squanto, the friend of the Pilgrims. His name had
other spellings. Of these, Tisquantum was most com-
monly used by those who met him in the New World
or in the Old between 1605 and 1620. The other four
Indians seized with him were Nahanada, Skitwarroes,
Assocomoit, and Maneday. They, too helped English
colonization but neither as directly nor as willingly as
Tisquantum did. Perhaps that is why we rarely hear
of them today.

For what we do know about them we must thank
two different kinds of men. First, of course, are the
adventurers and colonizers themselves who dealt with
them. These were men like James Rosier, William
Bradford, and Captain John Smith. In the midst of
dangers and hardships, these men and others took
time to jot down in journals or letters what they saw
and what they did. To them it was important
that their fellow Englishmen should know about the
lands across the sea. But those who preserved many

of their stories so that we can read them today were of another sort from these men of action.

They never sailed to the new lands but gathered the stories of those who did and had them published. Richard Hakluyt was such an editor. He did not collect these accounts only because of his interest in geography and adventure. He thought the stories had a message for the English people.

His country must have colonies, he felt. He saw other countries of Europe, particularly Spain, England's bitter rival, enriching themselves from their colonies. He saw his own nation in the grip of hard times. Hundreds of strong and worthy men were out of work. They starved to death in the city streets. They stole to feed their families, and many were hung for these petty thefts. If only England could plant colonies, Hakluyt insisted, she could soon become wealthy as other nations had and, at the same time, provide places where her people could find work.

It was to let his countrymen know about the vast lands being explored that Hakluyt worked so hard. Whenever an expedition was ready to sail, he badgered some one of its members to keep a record of the adventure. Whenever one returned, he himself took down word by word from the lips of its seamen their stories. During these same years he traveled over rough roads from one end of England to the other to gather accounts, already written, dating back to the very first days of exploration. He had the tales, both old and new, published together so that the English people could read them and know of the tremendous future for colonies. Richard Hakluyt gave his collection a long title—*The Principal Navigations, Voyages, Traffiques, and Discoveries of the English Nation.* By 1600 he had published all of these tales that he was going to and another editor took over many that he had not used.

This editor was Samuel Purchas. He called his collection *Purchas his Pilgrimes* and added to the sea tales and land travel stories that he had had gathered himself many that Hakluyt had not printed.

In the pages of these books we meet the Indian as he was when the white man first found him. We see him before he was given guns and "strong water" and before he was caught up in quarrels that had their beginnings far over the seas. His hunting lands and cornfields had not yet been taken from him after he had signed land-deeds which he did not understand. (An Indian had no idea of land ownership as the English understood it. Whenever he signed away his land by making his mark upon a piece of paper, he thought that he was merely giving his new friends permission to use these vast acres as he himself used them. He expected his lands to be kept open and free for roaming hunters in the Indian way.)

Time and time again we read in the old accounts of the warm welcome the savages gave the first newcomers. As the ships passed close inshore, the natives ran along the rocky ledges at the water's edge, leaping and dancing a joyous greeting, or launched their birch canoes and paddled out to overtake the white-winged vessels. It took only a few years for the men from overseas to change all this by their harsh treatment of the Indians.

When the old accounts were written by the early voyagers to the New World, the people of England and Europe were living in stirring times, full of new wonders. At last adventurers had gotten beyond the natural barriers of sea and mountains that enclosed their lands. Then, as greater skills in navigation and shipbuilding developed, many could venture where before only a hardy few had dared to go. They could visit other parts of the globe and see other of their fellow creatures. They could look upon faces different from their own, observe strange ways of living, and wonder what was yet to be found.

Nowadays we think that we have seen all the peoples of the earth. We have not always met them first hand, to be sure, but in photographs that reach us in books, magazines, on the screen and television, or in carefully written accounts. Unless a new race springs from some chasm in the earth's crust, we have seen all its inhabitants.

In the days of Queen Elizabeth and King James of England, however, it was still a time of wonder and surprise. Then a boy living in one of the English ports could run to the docks at the cry of "Sail ho!" and expect to see strange and wonderful sights. Likely as not there would be visitors aboard the anchoring vessel, men undreamed of from other lands—men with rings in their ears or bones thrust through their cheeks, men wearing almost no clothes or wrapped to the ears in furs. One never knew what to expect. If there were no strangers to stare at, there still was the pleasure of listening to sailors' yarns about distant lands. And perhaps the next ship might bring in odder creatures than any yet seen—men who were half horse, or who had one eye in the middle of their foreheads, such as were described in the ancient tales.

It was in those days of wonder and expectation that there came into England's Plymouth Harbor in the summer of 1605 a bark bearing five kidnapped Indians from the New England coast. Why the savages had been brought to England and what happened to them afterward is the concern of this book.

FIVE KIDNAPPED INDIANS

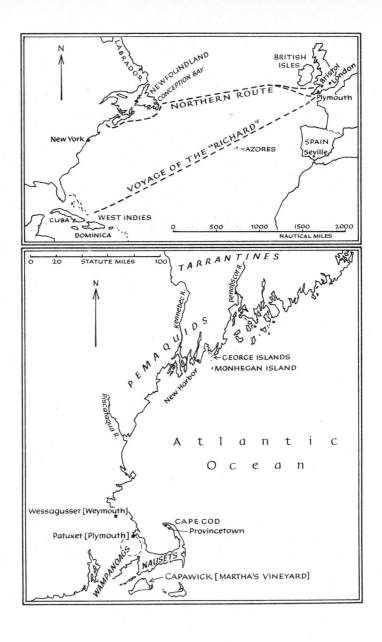

CHAPTER ONE

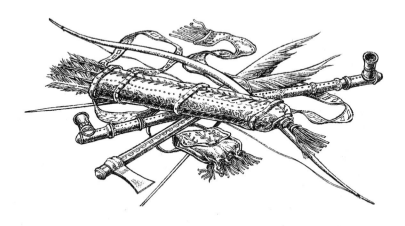

CAPTAIN GEORGE WAYMOUTH was feeling more and more uneasy. In this June of 1605 he had already been twelve days off the coast of North Virginia, as New England was called then, and still he had seen no natives. And until he did, this long voyage from England by way of the Azores could not be called a success. To discover some savages and to carry them back home was its primary purpose. This was the reason so many English gentlemen of wealth had been

3

willing to invest money in fitting out the "Archangel," the bark which Captain Waymouth commanded.

None of the crewmen knew of the Captain's kidnapping intentions. It was a secret that he shared with but a few aboard—Master Thomas Cam, his mate, for one, and Master James Rosier, who was writing a record of the voyage.

Owen Griffith knew the secret, too. He was the young man who had made a courageous promise to stay behind in the New World when the "Archangel" sailed for England if no savages could be taken. He would live alone on this rocky coast to learn at first hand what the country had to offer. He would study it for colony sites and mineral wealth. Then the next year, when another vessel was sent out, he would be picked up. That is, if he survived. The climate of this coast was unknown and the nature of the "salvages," as the English of those days called the Indians, was little known.

To kidnap several natives and question them about their country would, of course, be a quicker way to find out important facts. It would mean that a colony could be sent out the following spring instead of a year later. And it would make Captain Waymouth's voyage in the "Archangel" a success. The Captain was doubly eager that it should be because his last expedition had ended in failure.

Three years before, in 1602, he had been sent to find the rumored Northwest Passage to the Orient, a short cut to the fabled riches of the East. The paper on which Captain Waymouth's men signed on for that voyage still exists. The signatures of the seamen and the marks of those who could not write are still plain on its surface. So, too, are the lists of supplies and clothing necessary for the northerly regions through which they must pass—leather breeches furred with white lambskin, leather cassocks and hoods to fasten to them, warm mittens—clothes not too different from those worn by Admiral Peary and his men when they set out for the discovery of the North Pole in 1909. One of the greater expenses of Captain Waymouth's voyage was that of having a letter copied from Queen Elizabeth to "the Right High Mighty and Invincible Emperor of Cathay." It must be suitably penned and illuminated with gold and colored capital letters to carry the Virgin Queen's greetings to the Oriental potentate.

This 1602 expedition of Captain Waymouth's set out across the Atlantic from London and ran into mountainous ice barriers off the Labrador coast. At one time both of its vessels were in danger of being crushed among four great islands of ice which Waymouth said were "of a huge bigness." From the direction of the shore they heard, like the crack of a gun, the terrifying report that follows a break in the ice. It was, he recorded, "very loathsome to be heard." Soon the vessels' sails and rigging were frozen stiff. The craft became almost unmanageable and the crew, in terror, began to mutiny. Captain Waymouth, however, was more fortunate than Henry Hudson, whose mutinous men were to turn him adrift among the ice floes some years later. Perhaps Waymouth had a wisdom that enabled him to handle his men better; in any case, he ended the mutiny and, heeding the clamor of his crew, sailed for home.

This ignominious end to his search for the Northwest Passage and Cathay naturally made Waymouth most eager for the success of his voyage in the "Archangel" to North Virginia. He sailed from Ratcliffe, on the Thames near London, on March 5, 1605.

Everything the Captain did on this voyage justified the trust of the men who put him in command. James Rosier wrote a record of it which he called his *Relation*. In it he said, "I cannot omit the painful industry of our captain, who at sea he is always most careful and vigilant, so at land he refuseth no pains; but his labor was ever as much or more than any man's."

In fact, the Captain was so vigilant in carrying out the orders he had been given that he was put down as a villain by later readers. It is rather unfortunate that the account of Rosier, who admired Waymouth, should have helped him win this bad name. But there it is among Rosier's pages, the working out of the evil kidnapping plot. Gradually the reader comes to realize what the return cargo of the "Archangel" was intended from the first to be: not sassafras root or furs, the two most sought-after cargoes of those years, but a mysterious commodity that at first is not mentioned openly in the record. When Rosier speaks of the good qualities of some of the natives, it is apparent that the Captain plans to freight a human cargo. Rosier tells how together they set the trap for the Indians and then sprung it.

The "Archangel" had cruised and lain for twelve days along what is now the coast of Maine before Captain Waymouth could get about the business of the voyage. Although he fretted at the delay, this was a pleasant time for his crew. On Monhegan Island, twelve miles off the mainland, they went ashore for the first feeling of firm ground beneath their feet in many weeks. They drank fresh water from a spring and rolled out driftwood for the cook's fire from the tangle of morning-glory vines and beach peas above the curve of white beach. Those who stayed aboard the "Archangel" dropped lines over the side and soon had large codfish flapping on the deck—fresh food to replace the salt meat and dry biscuit on which they had lived for so long. But they saw no Indians.

Soon, to be nearer the mainland, they moved to the Georges Islands and dropped anchor among them. On several they went ashore and cut wood for the cook's fires. They scoured out springs to make the water clear. They even dug the ground and planted the barley and peas brought from home for a trial of this soil. Soon the seeds sprouted and began to grow. And still no Indians.

Finally, the Captain called James Rosier to his small, low-ceilinged cabin high up in the ship's stern and laid a plan before him. He proposed to call in some savages as hunters do migratory birds. He would give orders for the vessel's saker to be fired in the hope of attracting their attention. Now a saker is only a small cannon taking six-pound shot, but on a calm day such as this it could be heard for miles.

Rosier, said the Captain, was to stay aboard with some crewmen. They were to deal with any visitors whose curiosity might be aroused by the cannon's report. He himself would man the shallop, their open, two-masted boat, to "discover along the coast" and find whatever rivers trended into the mainland. One might prove to be the Northwest Passage to Cathay.

And the shallop party might come upon some savages as well.

Waymouth gave orders for the saker to be fired. The gunner's eyes sparkled and all the crew brightened. They were young again when this form of celebrating was in prospect. The cabin boy, whose name we are never told by Rosier, was beside himself with excitement. This almost made up for his not being chosen a member of the Captain's exploring party!

The gunner allowed the cabin boy to light the fuse. While the flame crept slowly toward the powder pan, the lad kept his hands over his ears and watched with nervous excitement. Whenever the saker was fired, there was always the possibility of its bronze sides bursting.

With a flash the charge exploded. The little cannon reared back in recoil like a terrified horse on its haunches. The roar echoed back from the islands' dark headlands.

"Give them three to fetch them in," the captain had ordered.

Three times the martial music boomed.

It was hours later before three canoes slipped past the "Archangel" in answer to its call. There were ten naked paddlers in each of the birch craft. Two carried women and children. As silent and unseeing as people in a dream they glided past and made for the nearest island. Here they beached their canoes and soon had a fire blazing on the shore.

Then the mate, Master Cam, called out to the crew, "Raise your caps and waft them to us, lads."

The men waved and hallooed. No reply came from the savages.

The men called again, and this time they had a response. One of the three canoes, with three Indians aboard, put out.

At last the evil plan, begun in England so many months ago, was working out!

CHAPTER TWO

ON THE MORNING of that same day three Pemaquid squaws trudged toward their homes as fast as their burdens allowed. Their village was on the far side of the rocky point which faced out across a bay to Waymouth's island anchorage. The three women were bent double beneath dripping baskets of lobsters which they had spent the morning gathering. Most of the time they had been waist-deep in frigid water, diving down when they saw one of the green, speckled creatures crawling among the rocks on the sea bottom, and then bobbing up with the crusty prize. They knew how to hold the lobsters close to the base of their claws, safe from the creatures' cruel grip.

At last the women came to the Indians' cornfields, which were kept neat by their clam-shell hoes. They gave scarcely a glance to the tender green V's of the young corn as they passed. They went on and stopped before a cluster of bent-sapling houses and slid their burdens from their backs. As soon as they could straighten up, they hurried to Nahanada. He was their sagamore, their king. They must tell him at once of the terrifying sight they had seen, of the strange thunder they had heard. If any harm came to the Pemaquids from it, the squaws would be blamed for not giving the warning.

For some time they had known where to find the sagamore, Nahanada. The shouts of, "Hub, hub, hub" as the men played one of their favorite games could be heard many paces from the village. Before the women had made their early start in the morning, the game had been under way. The men played on the bare, hard-packed ground in the center of the village. Even then, with the sun scarcely above the horizon, five or six beaver cloaks had changed owners with the fall of the black and white bones in the wooden platter.

For several days Tisquantum, of the Patuxets,

who lived far down the coast, beyond even the Massachusetts tribe and the Great Blue Hill, had been visiting in the settlement. His people were allied with the Pemaquids against their common enemy to the north, the dreaded Tarrantines. Tisquantum and all his people were always welcome here. There had been feasting in his honor and a football game that had lasted for two days.

Now the women approached the players. The young squaw who was the wife of Skitwarroes saw her own cloak lying beside their guest, Tisquantum. In her fright and worry at what she had seen this morning, she scarcely mourned its loss. She had lost others when the gaming fever was on her husband, and she knew that he would trap more beaver for another cloak. Her thoughts were all on the difficulty of telling Nahanada and the other braves her story. And she must tell it, even though she got nothing more than blows for her pains. If only the men would listen and not brush her words aside as quickly as they might a louse or a flea from an ear!

When the women came near, Skitwarroes was holding the wooden platter of bones. He beat his breast with one clenched fist and cried, "Hub, hub, hub!" With both hands he brought down the platter against the ground. He did it again and again with such force that the bones leaped and turned in midair. Many that had had a black side on top now presented a white one.

"Hub, hub, hub," roared the other men.

In the first moment of quiet, Skitwarroes' wife spoke up. "We saw it with our own eyes, an island that moved," she said quickly. Then she dodged back lest any blow might come her way for this interruption of the game.

"A walking island, with bare trees upon it," said another of the women, who then retreated also.

"And from that walking island with bare trees upon it came thunder and lightning," said the third squaw.

The men paid no attention. Their guest, Tisquantum, held the platter now. All eyes were upon him as he shouted, "Hub, hub, hub."

The three squaws looked at each other for courage to go on. Skitwarroes' wife gained it first.

Once more she bravely stepped forward and said, "And from that walking island came thunder and lightning, although the sun shone in the sky. What kind of magic was this? We came to tell you at once, lest harm for your people be on the way."

At last Nahanada heard the fear in her voice and heeded it. Because he was sagamore, he must think of the safety of his people as well as the hospitality due their guest. He held up one hand to stop the game.

"Tell us again what your eyes have seen and your ears have heard," he said with his usual calm dignity.

Again the women told their story.

When they had finished, Tisquantum, their guest, said, "It is the white men come back again from their homes across the water. Two times the spring tides have risen since they came to the Patuxets. They came to our village in their great canoes with white wings. They came with fierce and long-legged dogs. They filled their canoes with roots of the sassafras tree. Then they sailed away again."

"Are they friend or foe, these white men?" asked Nahanada.

"They can be either," said Tisquantum.

The hub-hub game was forgotten. The sagamore gave orders for two of the women to guide him and some of his braves to where they had seen the thundering ship. Other squaws at once took the rush mats from several houses and began to roll them for the men to carry with them. They might need shelter before they returned. First the squaws took off the weathered outside mats from the bent-sapling house frames. Then they took down the brightly decorated mats hanging inside. They carried these with the wall and roof mats down to three large canoes drawn up upon the shore. Under the crafts' great up-curving beaks they stowed them with fur sleeping mats and leather bags holding corn meal and tobacco.

Before long the three canoes, two of them carrying a woman and her youngest child, had left the river mouth for the bay. They rounded the high rocky point, swung to the east and swept into that other bay where the women had seen the white men's ship. Soon they were able to make out its bare masts and to hear the *chink-chink-chink* and *thunk-thunk* of woodcutters at work on one of the islands.

Nahanada had told his braves what the plan of action was. All three canoes were to paddle past the vessel, and the Indians were to allow themselves to be seen landing on the nearest island. They would ignore the white men and the ship with its mouths that could send out thunder and lightning. Let the strangers give the first sign. Then perhaps they could tell whether they were friend or foe.

The women, although they knew the force of the guns, sat as calmly as the thirty braves in the canoes. They kept their eyes on the paddlers' backs, whose muscles moved to the same rhythm.

Silently the canoes glided past the ship. The paddlers made for the shingle cove on the nearest island and beached the canoes.

At once Nahanada ordered the squaws to gather firewood. Assocomoit, one of the braves, he told to build a fire.

Assocomoit took a small leather bag from his snakeskin belt. From it he brought out a flat emery stone tied to a little stick, a flint, and a piece of touchwood. Gently he struck the flint with the emery stone until sparks flew from it and fell down upon the touchwood. He blew on the sparks, and when they ignited he heaped dried leaves and twigs upon the touchwood. Soon he had a merry blaze going which the women were to feed and build up into a good fire.

The other men stood about waiting, holding their bone-tipped harpoons. Nahanada had planned that their expedition should have the appearance of a porpoise hunt. They did not look directly toward the near-by ship, but they were completely aware of everything happening on its deck. Not one of them missed seeing the white men raise their hats and wave a greeting. The braves looked toward Nahanada for him to say what their next step would be.

The sagamore watched the beckoning men in motionless silence. His decision was an important one, he knew. After a time he said, "Skitwarroes and Assocomoit, since a sagamore can not go to visitors before they come to him, you will go to these white men for me. Tisquantum, who knows their ways, will go too. Ask them what it is they want of us."

The three Indians pushed off one of the canoes and were soon paddling it toward the anchored vessel.

CHAPTER THREE

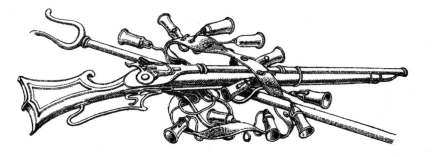

As the three Indians skimmed toward the "Arch-angel" in their canoe, Master Rosier spoke to the crewmen watching with him from the vessel. "At long last our work of bringing light to the savages can commence," he remarked piously.

None of the rest said a word. The three natives were so awesomely painted that even those who had been with Sir Walter Raleigh and had seen many savages in the Indies and along the Orinoco River were silent. The cabin boy moved closer to Owen Griffith even while he thought, "Here at last is something to tell the town when I go home to London again."

The Indians were naked except for beaver-skin breech clouts tucked, with a flap back and front, through their snakeskin belts. Their long hair was clubbed up with leather thongs, and feathers were woven into the black strands. Their faces were as brilliantly painted as the masks worn in a mummers' procession. One face was striped with blue and one with red. One was a solid black. All had eyebrows drawn on with white paint.

The Indian in the stern, whose head was bound with a red fillet, raised his paddle. He pointed toward the open sea and called out in a fierce voice as if he were a landowner ordering trespassers from his fields. None of the Englishmen understood his guttural words, but his meaning was clear: "Tell us why you came here, and then leave if you mean no good!"

Instead of answering, Master Cam carried out the Captain's orders. He had had one of the sailors bring up a great sack from the hold. Now he reached into it and brought out various of the trading articles that it held. As he distributed them among the crew —mirrors and knives, whistles and peacock feathers —he told the men to make them attractive to the savages.

It was the cabin boy who first caught the Indians'

interest. He remembered how his schoolmates had plagued the schoolmaster with just such an innocent weapon as one of these mirrors. He took the round bit of mirrored glass that he had been given, caught a beam of sunlight with it, and reflected it straight into the eyes of the red-filleted savage.

The Indian sat rigid. Perhaps he thought that he had been hit by some weapon and was waiting for a roar of thunder to follow, or for pain. Again the boy tipped his mirror and caught the savage's eye with a beam. This time the straight stripes across the grim face curved with a smile.

Meanwhile the other crewmen were at work. One whittled a stick in great slashes with a gleaming new knife. Another flaunted a peacock feather invitingly. Every man beckoned welcome, and gradually the canoe inched closer.

Finally the Indians were just below the bark's rail and the three young braves were climbing the ship's ladder. Skitwarroes, Assocomoit, and Tisquantum had decided that the Englishmen were not foes but friends.

Then Prince and Polly, the two great mastiff dogs who had the run of the ship, almost spoiled the confidence the crew had built up in their visitors. They growled menacingly as these men who smelled so unlike Englishmen strode across the deck.

The Indians hesitated, turned, and ran back to the rail with the mastiffs at their heels.

"Tie up the beasts!" Master Cam ordered.

Two sailors seized the dogs by their collars and fastened them to their hutch chains.

The savages stayed. It wasn't long before each had a peacock feather waving among the turkey feathers in his hair. No peacock was ever prouder than these braves when they looked into their gift mirrors and beheld for the first time their own ferocious faces and their iridescent feathers. With respectful fingers they touched the blades of their new knives.

"Oh-ho," they said over and over, showing their pleasure with a particular present.

Master Cam sent the cabin boy below for food. The cook, up on deck to see the sights, ran down with him to the cooking-place. From a steaming kettle he ladled three pewter bowlfuls of pease porridge. He heaped a pewter plate with ship's biscuit. The boy seized that, the cook came with the bowls, and back up on deck again they raced. Neither wanted to miss a minute of their strange visitors' antics.

At first the Indians were puzzled by the biscuit. They found it a curious food, hard and dry, although they ate it. The porridge they liked at once.

They spooned it up and blew cooling gusts into each hot green spoonful.

Before they paddled back to the island, they gave Master Cam a fine beaver skin and, with nods and beckonings, invited him to come the next day to trade with them.

When Captain Waymouth returned from his scouting along the coast he learned that his trap had been baited.

Very pleased, he sent a party ashore the next day to repay the Indians' visit. Master Cam led them, and Owen Griffith went because the more he knew of savage ways the better. He would need to know a great deal if he was to stay behind when the "Archangel" left. The shore party was instructed to carry on trading as though they had no other purpose in this country.

The cabin boy strained his eyes after the men when they set out for the island the next morning. The hours dragged past for him until the mate and Owen came into the Captain's cabin to report. The boy was serving the Captain his dinner. He stretched the meal out in order not to miss a word of what the two had to say.

"They had not over many skins for trading," said Master Cam, "but what they had we got at a most fair rate, for trifles. Forty beaver skins we got, and

otter and others. When we conjectured yesterday
that he of the red fillet is one of their principal
men, we were correct. He is called Skitwarroes. One
of the others was a servant, the second a friend visiting from another nation. Nahanada, their chief,
sends to you a bag of their savage tobacco. It is
quite the finest I have ever puffed. And you will not
have to try it as we did, turn and turn about with
the savages, from a lobster-claw pipebowl and sitting
the while upon a deerskin. Withal, they treated us
most civilly."

Here Owen took up the account. "Ah, Captain, you
would have split your sides with laughing to see
them devour the meat we carried to them and,
when they came upon the mustard and felt the full
bite of its strength, pull the sourest faces you can
conceive."

Owen pulled his own face into the proper grimace,
and added, "Their young chieftain, Nahanada by
name, comes to sup with you on the morrow."

Owen told of catching a fleeting glimpse of the
two squaws. They had hurried out of sight when the
English arrived and had shooed their two little
boys ahead of them. The women wore fine beaver
skins, splendid enough to pay the debts of one of
King James' courtiers, and yet they tied them about
their middles as though they were kitchenmaids'

aprons. As for the young ones, they were naked as
the day they were born, except for long leather leg-
gings to keep their legs from scratches.

By this time the Captain had finished eating,
and the cabin boy had no excuse to linger in the
cabin. He gathered up the dirty dishes to take them
to the cooking-place. He went out on deck, and as
he stepped down from the poop he saw the gleam of
birch-bark canoes putting out from the island. They
were making for the "Archangel!"

The boy went back to notify the Captain before
he ran below.

"Stir up the pot, Cook," he called out when he
reached the galley. "There be guests a-coming, three
canoes, and full of painted savages."

"Oh, aye, I'll stir it," said Cook, with a groan,
"but please to remind the Captain that my pots
have bottoms to 'em. If this lot eats as did yesterday's three, it's bottomless pots we'll be needing,
I'm thinking. And so it goes for me. Up on deck
there will be as much mirth and merriment as at a
Thames-side bear-baiting and where will Cook be
all that time? Alone, below."

Cook was wrong about this last. Soon the deck
about his feet in the cooking-place was filled with
Indians sitting cross-legged. He had barely room to
step as he ladled out and filled bowl after bowl

with green pease porridge. The Captain sent the boy below to fetch three servings of pork and biscuits and pease porridge. Two among the guests he had singled out for special treatment. Why, the boy couldn't tell; they looked no different from the other savages. But when he saw the Captain eating again so soon with the two, the boy knew that something was afoot. Did the Captain feel that these two could lead him to the Northwest Passage, to the back side of America, where the wealth of the world was waiting?

The two were Nahanada, the sagamore, and his cousin, Skitwarroes.

After the meal was done, Captain Waymouth pressed them to spend the night aboard the "Archangel." Nahanada refused for them both. He made signs to show that as sagamore he must stay with his people. Three others might remain, he said, if one of the English went ashore with him as a hostage.

Owen Griffith, of course, was the one chosen to sleep with the savages. The sailors who had been in the Indies and knew the natives there shook their heads and told Owen that he was taking his life in his hands by going. As a perfectly full moon slid smiling up into the sky, Owen went ashore with Nahanada, and the boy felt awe at the man's courage.

The three Indians chosen to sleep aboard picked themselves a sleeping spot on deck. For some reason this did not suit the Captain. To the crew's amazement he took them below to the orlop deck, the lowest of all, and saw them bedded down on an old sail.

The sun was scarcely up before the Indians found their way up on deck again and pointed to the shore. They wanted to return to their friends at once. They were ferried across in the ship's boat, which brought Owen back on its return. Already strange reports of doings ashore had been circulated by the night's watch, and the crew gathered about Owen as he came aboard.

"Tell us, Owen, tell us about their pranks and antics. The watch, he heard them at it all night long. Fairly like day it was by the light of the moon, he said. Tell us," they clamored.

Owen shook his head mysteriously and went to the Captain's cabin. He shut the door to the curious.

The Captain was the first to hear his story.

"For aught I know, Sir," said Owen, "our friends ashore have some correspondency with the Devil and were busy at it when I arrived. A pow-wow is what they called their antics last night, at least."

He spoke jokingly, but through his words the strain under which he had been still showed.

"A short night for you, I fear," said the Captain, "and for me. The man on watch was not the only one to hear strange clamorings. Do end my suspense and imaginings and tell me what you saw."

"It began," answered Owen, "with the eldest of them rising up before the others assembled and crying loudly, 'Baugh-waugh.' Flat the two women fell upon their faces as if not privileged to see such mysteries. The men chorused, 'Baugh-waugh,' and fell a-stamping 'round about the fire and making the very ground to shake. Sundry outcries they gave with changes of voice and sound."

Owen paused to chuckle at his memories, and then resumed.

"They took burning brands from out of the campfire and thrust them into the ground, then rested for awhile when, lo, as suddenly as before they fell to stamping again, till the younger sort fetched from the shore many stones, of which every man took one. First, they beat upon the abused earth with their fire sticks, then with the stones they beat it with all their strength. After two hours, without warning the hellish scene ended, and the men and women went to rest. As for me, I lay wondering till almost dawn."

Later Owen was persuaded to tell the crew of his experiences. It was Sunday and a day of rest for them all. They had time to talk over the pow-wow and to wonder what it might mean. Was it simply a ceremony that was always held when the moon was full? Or were the savages working a magic against the English? Many of the men felt that this was so and that they should be more on their guard against the Indians.

In spite of this feeling among the crew, the Captain showed no concern when a dark and distant speck upon the bay became a canoe. He turned his glass upon it and when the light craft drew alongside, he welcomed aboard its crew of strange savages.

CHAPTER FOUR

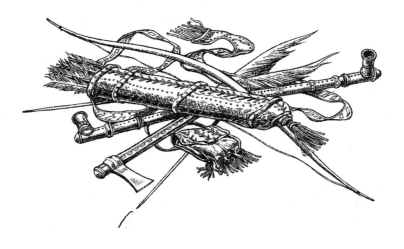

THE STRANGERS HAD COME to the "Archangel"
from Bashaba, the great sagamore.

Nahanada had sent off one of his men to the
mainland not many hours after he and Captain
Waymouth had their first meeting. The brave was
carrying a message to Bashaba: Men from over the
sea were here in a great, white-winged canoe. They
were eager to give bright feathers and sharp knives
and pieces of glass that showed a man what his eye
alone could not see in exchange for beaver skins.

The messenger followed the tidal stream on whose banks he had been left by a canoe and ran along well-trodden Indian trails to Bashaba. His orders were to stop for nothing until he reached his journey's end. On he jogged. He stopped only to drink from a stream when it ran clear from its source or to take a palmful of *nocake,* the meal ground from parched corn, from his leather pouch and mix it to an edible paste with the water.

Now, although Nahanada was a sagamore with the power of a king in his Pemaquid tribe, he recognized Bashaba as one of his overlords. Among his own people he could demand obedience and, with his council, he could sentence offenders to a quick death by tomahawk, club, or knife. He could demand a certain share of the Pemaquids' crops and of the game they killed, and he could be certain that at his death his son, or even his daughter, would inherit all these rights. But, powerful as he was, Nahanada obeyed Bashaba.

The great overlord protected him from his enemies. In return, he demanded the Pemaquids as allies whenever he made war. He expected to be informed of all that went on in their part of the country.

In fact, not only Nahanada but all the sagamores

between the Penobscot River to the northeast and the Piscataqua to the south were bound to Bashaba by the same ties. He was their shield against the plundering, murdering Tarrantines, who lived still farther north. The thought of these dangerous neighbors always hung in the minds of the coastal tribes like a dark cloud perpetually upon the horizon. Because Bashaba was strong enough to stand up to the Tarrantines, his name was spoken with great respect by his Indian allies. It was this that made Waymouth, and the English who visited these shores soon after, think that "Bashaba" was the native word for "king."

The Pemaquid who set out with Nahanada's message to Bashaba was fortunate. He soon came upon a corn-raising settlement and learned there that his journey was to be a short one; Bashaba was not in his villages far to the north, but at one only a few hours away.

There the Pemaquid delivered his message. Bashaba's response was eager. He would send a large party of his people with their best furs to trade with the newcomers at once. He himself would go, too, and they would meet the English sagamore at a certain cove in the nearest river on the mainland, a spot all the Pemaquids knew well. He dispatched one of his own canoes with paddlers to carry the messenger back with this word to Captain Waymouth.

Now it was neither the thought of acquiring bright feathers, mirrors, and knives nor idle curiosity that made his reply so enthusiastic. A wild hope had sprung up in Bashaba's heart.

He knew that other white men from a faraway country called France had visited the shores where the Tarrantines held sway. They had given his enemies bright brass kettles and a few of their muskets. Bashaba was not interested in getting more brass kettles from the Englishmen; his people already had some that had come down the coast from one hand to another. They were good kettles—so bright that one could see his face on the outside before soot from the fires dimmed them, so strong that a war club could not smash them—but he wanted guns. He knew well that unless his own people had muskets, the time would soon come when the Tarrantines would destroy them all. Their enemies were dangerous enough when they had only tomahawks and firebrands, but now that they had muskets they were doubly so. So Bashaba dispatched his canoe and braves to Captain Waymouth as the first step in acquiring the magic muskets of the white man.

His braves called at the island where the Pemaquids were staying. Then they paddled out to the "Archangel" and were welcomed aboard. They gave the Captain a fine beaver pelt and each brave was given in return a small cloth sack of bright beads and a dish of hot green soup. And after that they paddled off to tell Bashaba that the white saga-more's people would trade with him on the follow-ing day. At once Bashaba's village prepared to move to the meeting place and they soon were on the way.

Before the sun was overhead the next morning, two of Bashaba's men saw canoes coming toward the spot where they had set up their houses and where the blue-gray smoke of their fires rose above the peaked spruce trees. One canoe was a birch, the other a wide, heavy craft with a bare tree trunk standing in the middle and paddles reaching straight out from its sides. The Indian lookouts laughed to see the birch skimming ahead and then waiting for the other, or doubling back and circling it.

"The white man's canoe is an old dog, slow and moving straight; the Pemaquids' canoe is a young pup," said one.

When Bashaba was told that the canoes were coming, he felt an excitement that he did not show his people. Perhaps today he might obtain guns.

Perhaps he might obtain enough so that his warriors could slay the Tarrantines and rid themselves of that scourge forever.

He envied the ordinary braves now. They could race through the woods and look out from the shore at the strangers, but because he was a sagamore he must sit and await their coming. To pass the time he called some of the squaws and asked about their preparations for the feast. They must offer their visitors the finest of food. Did they have the proper amount of clams and sea birds and rabbits and wood pigeons boiling among the beans and *nocake* in their kettles? What flesh was roasting on the circles of spits ringing the fires? Were there bear steaks as well as venison? Satisfied that enough had been provided, he sent off a large number of his braves with their bows and arrows to welcome the English. He, himself, sat back to wait.

It was some time before the braves saw anyone start for shore; meanwhile, there was much talk between the men in the two canoes. Finally a bearded stranger exchanged places with one of the Pemaquids, and the birch canoe paddled toward the waiting braves. They met the white sagamore as he stepped onto the ledges.

Once he was ashore they learned that he was not the sagamore but his messenger, and that his name was Owen. He carried a long gun over his shoulder as he clambered up the ledges. Seeing it, the braves nervously put arrows to their bows.

"Where is the Bashaba?" asked Owen.

The braves pointed toward the cove where the sagamore, the feast, and the pile of fur pelts for trading waited.

"Bring Bashaba here," Owen ordered.

"You must go to Bashaba. He awaits you there," answered the braves.

Owen hesitated for only a moment. He shook his head angrily and ran back to the beached canoe. He pointed to his own canoe, where the sailors sat at their long paddles. "Take me back," he ordered the Pemaquids who had brought him ashore.

Bashaba's braves watched him being paddled away. They saw him exchange places again with the Indian who had taken his place in the white man's canoe. Then both craft turned and made for the islands from which they had come.

The braves stood wondering why the white men had not wanted to trade with them. Sadly they went to Bashaba with the bad news.

CHAPTER FIVE

OWEN GRIFFITH REPORTED to Captain Waymouth's cabin on the "Archangel" to tell him the story of the unsuccessful trading trip.

"I saw a plot, a ruse," he explained. "Here were gathered almost three hundred savages, and each man with his bow and arrow. I saw no evidence of stuff to be traded. They assured me that it all lay with Bashaba up a little nook in the river. Methinks there could as well have been a large party of their warriors waiting to fall upon us once they had us bottled up in that inlet."

He was so suspicious that Waymouth began to question whatever the savages did after that. Like so many men with bad intentions, he mistrusted those he intended to harm.

A week of lovely summer days passed with great activity. There was much visiting back and forth between the Pemaquids on the island and the men of the "Archangel." The Captain often invited Nahanada and Skitwarroes to sup with him. Afterwards he praised them to Rosier.

"These have intelligence and a ready capacity. These are the ones we most desire to bring with us to England," he would say.

In spite of the joking and laughing that went on when the two young Indians came to his cabin, mistrust was mounting on both sides. This made Captain Waymouth feel that the sooner he acted the better. If the Indians on the island took it into their heads to paddle away, all these days of patient, if false, friendliness would be wasted. He would be left holding a cage with his birds flown.

One morning he went ashore as usual with most of the crew to cut wood on one of the islands, but he left a new order. The gunner was to stay aboard the vessel and fire a musket if any of the Pemaquids came to call.

Before two hours had passed he heard the signal

above the chink of the axes. He sent James Rosier to the "Archangel" to entertain and detain, if need be, the Indians who had come aboard.

Rosier found two canoes alongside the vessel. The crew of one had gone aboard, but the others waited as if hopeful of being fed. He urged them to join him on the "Archangel," but they refused. When he went below to the cooking-place he found Tisquantum and Maneday enjoying a meal of peas and bread.

He dispatched the cabin boy with more bowls of peas and more bread for the men still in the canoe. They accepted the gift, but instead of eating at once they carried their meal ashore. Not long afterward Skitwarroes returned with the empty bowls. He came aboard and joined the other two Pemaquids below at the fire.

Captain Waymouth was right; something was afoot with the savages. Rosier ordered the six sailors who were passing the time of day with the Indians to seize them.

Immediately the sailors sprang upon their visitors. They soon had them bound and gagged and laid on the orlop deck. At the same time Rosier had others of the crew swing the two tell-tale canoes up over the side and carry them carefully down to the orlop. The birch craft with their paddles still in

place and with several bows and arrows under the beaks would be of great interest to the curious in England.

It all happened almost as quickly as it can be told. Any of the Indians on the island who might have looked out and seen the canoes bobbing along-side the vessel would look again and rub their eyes and think that they had been mistaken.

Soon the Captain came in answer to the musket's call. He praised Rosier for carrying out his part of the plan so well. They agreed that the rest must be done at once, before the captives were missed by their friends on the island. Rosier had several crew-men lower a chest of trading trinkets into the ship's boat. With them he went ashore.

The Englishmen looked first for Nahanada, the prize most worth seizing. They found him with As-socomoit and another Indian at the campfire. Even before Rosier could get the trading chest open, how-ever, this unnamed brave disappeared among the brush as if he sensed danger. Rosier knew that he must hurry, but he took time to go through the mo-tions of trading, like a door-to-door peddler dis-playing his wares. He brought out whistles and blew them temptingly for comparison of their tones and dangled blue beads enticingly. If the third Indian saw or heard, he gave no sign of returning.

Finally Rosier gave more orders in a tone as calm as if he were predicting the morrow's weather. He didn't want to alarm their prey.

"Two of these birds are better than none. We must act at once or lose that bird the Captain wants most," he said, and gave the signal.

Seven sailors sprang upon the two savages.

Nahanada and his companion were both young and both were fighting for their lives. Time after time they almost escaped. Their naked bodies were slippery with bear grease. Finally, it was the Indians' long hair that proved their undoing. One sailor was able to hold tight to each black club as if he had a lion by the tail while his mates trussed and gagged the two savages. Soon Nahanada and Assocomoit were lying with the three other captives deep down on the orlop deck.

The prisoners were most probably locked into bilboes, an ingenious set of sliding shackles that could secure a row of prisoners with only one lock. Bilboes got their name from Bilbao in Spain, and many a seagoing vessel carried them in those days. There was no telling when they might be needed for mutinous sailors, pirates, or other prisoners.

For a week after the kidnapping the "Archangel" stayed in these same waters. Remarkably, none of the Pemaquids on shore raised a hue and cry for their missing sagamore and tribesmen.

Now the English tried to shun the Indians whom they had courted so eagerly. Once two canoes carrying savages paddled up to the "Archangel." Immediately Captain Waymouth and his men were on the defensive. This was the day of reckoning; now they must suffer for their deed, they thought.

But the savages were strangers. They had come from Bashaba, who still wanted to trade with the English. They pointed to where Bashaba awaited them with his furs.

They had to take "No" for an answer. This didn't satisfy the Indians, however. They wanted to come aboard the "Archangel" and see its wonders.

Master Cam ordered the dogs chained, and the visitors clambered over the side. The English entertained the Indians warily, as if they might somehow be able to see through the decking planks down into the orlop.

When at last they paddled away, the English heaved sighs of relief.

"After this, no more savages aboard of us," ordered the Captain. "Let the mastiffs roam at will and the creatures will have too much fear of them to risk a visit. Bashaba can carry his furs to the

French for all of us; our business with the savages is done, praise be! Now let us get on with our unfinished business."

Both captain and crew hurried uneasily through what remained to be done. Enough firewood for the voyage must be cut and stored, their search for the Northwest Passage must be carried on, the exact position of the harbor where they lay and the depths within it must be recorded. The safety of those who came after them from England might depend on this information.

The captain was a man of peace. He had no desire for an encounter with enraged relatives of his captives, but he must risk this danger for one more trip of exploration on the mainland.

He ordered his shackled prisoners to be gagged lest they make an outcry that could be heard ashore. The "Archangel's" anchor came up over the side and they sailed up a tidal river until it became too shallow for the bark. Then a party of sailors took to the ship's boat, the pinnace, and went on.

As the salt-crusted marsh grass gave way to leafy banks, the hot sun brought out the scent of wild roses and pines. The men landed and started to walk toward the round blue hills which they had first sighted when they were still well out to sea on the voyage over. In spite of the heat the Captain and his men traveled not only fully armed but in armor as well.

This time the cabin boy was in the shore party. He went along to carry powder and match for the flintlock guns that so impressed the Indians whenever they heard them fired. The boy wore a bandolier, a shoulder strap from which hung a row of small wooden bottles. Each bottle carried enough powder for a charge. He wore the match, a long piece of tow, around his hat as a good musketeer's man always did until he should be ordered to light its two ends for use.

It was a parching hot trip. The country between them and the hills danced with heat waves. On they marched, mile after mile, the men miserable in their armor. The hills turned from the blue of distance to green, and yet they were still far away when the men turned back toward the ship.

As they traveled the sailors praised the fair meadows and the stately trees. They confessed that in spite of this being heathen country they would just as soon settle in it and lay their bones here. And although they enjoyed the feel of firm ground beneath their feet, they had never been so hot and thirsty before. Back home the sun did not stare a body as straight in the eye as it did here.

Later, when they had returned to England, the Captain told his employers that this splendid river (many think that it was the St. George) which they had followed could lead to the South Sea. The men who had explored its banks with him on that hot day were surprised to hear this. He had not mentioned this possibility then. Perhaps he made this claim about the river merely to satisfy his employers, Lord Wardour and others, that he *had* searched for the Northwest Passage.

Toward the middle of June the crew filled the "Archangel's" water casks with cold island water and the ship set sail for home. To the men, this seemed a sudden retreat. They had ample supplies for a much longer stay, and the best weather and the longest days of the year were yet to come. Why didn't they stay on and cruise along the coast and fill the hold with more beaver pelts than the few they had bartered from the Pemaquids?

Captain Waymouth knew the answer, even though his men did not. The wealthy gentlemen for whom he was making the voyage were more interested in future riches from gold mines than in present and lesser wealth from furs. Like all Europeans, they were aware that the Spaniards had carried fabulous cargoes of gold and silver from their possessions in the New World. It was no secret that in only thirteen years—from 1587 to 1600—their carricks had creaked across the Atlantic from Porto Bello or Havana to Seville with a million and a half dollars' worth of treasure. The English hoped to find sources of ore as valuable as the Spaniards' in the part of the New World that had been considered theirs since John Cabot's voyage of discovery in 1497.

Now, when they had kidnapped five intelligent natives from the English New World to question about sources of mineral wealth, there was a chance that they could find gold. Captain Waymouth knew that although Lord Wardour and the others might talk briskly about sending the "Archangel" to spread Christianity, to establish colonies, or gather furs, first and foremost it was these Indians and their knowledge that they wanted. He knew that his second voyage to America was a success.

It was to be his last trip to those shores, however. Thereafter he sailed to the eastward with the English pepper fleets. The English were seeking to wrest some of the spice trade away from the Portugese. Ever since her sailors had explored the Indian and Arabian coasts, Portugal had had this trade to herself.

As for the five Indians, Nahanada, Tisquantum, Skitwarroes, Maneday, and Assocomoit, they could only wonder whether they would see their native shores again. As they lay shackled on the dark, air-less orlop deck they might well have thought de-spairingly that this creaking, rolling prison would be theirs forever.

CHAPTER SIX

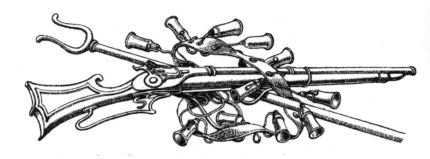

BEFORE THE VOYAGE was over, Captain Waymouth allowed his prisoners to come up on deck. One day, more than a month after the "Archangel" had sailed, Nahanada and the other four were sitting cross-legged outside the captain's door. They had been there from the time that the Scilly Island ledges had risen like great haystacks from the sea. Their keen eyes made out the faint lavender line of the Cornish coast long before the sailors could. Now, in the long English twilight, they were entering Plymouth Harbor. They were eager to step ashore and be among the green fields they saw not far distant.

"King James his country is green, much green," the five kept repeating.

Captain Waymouth had explained to the sagamore why he had carried them off like slaves. They were to be borrowed from their native land, but only for a short time. When they had learned enough English to answer questions about their country for King James' men, back they would sail again to their own people. Perhaps they would be aboard the very first vessel to leave England for North Virginia.

Nahanada had explained it all to his kinsmen as they still lay in their dark prison below decks. They had agreed that the faster they learned to speak the King's tongue the sooner they might be home again. And once the Captain had allowed them to be freed from their shackles so that they could come up into the fresh salt air, they had set to work with great eagerness. They snatched hungrily at every English word they heard. They tried to get their tongues, which they felt must be of a different shape from English ones, around the hard words. They even taught words of their own speech to any sailor interested enough to ask the Pemaquid way of saying this or that. They taught the night watch their names for the moon and the stars in the summer skies.

They had agreed, too, to be merry. Mourning for home would not get them back over those waters on which they had been sailing for more than a moon. So why not be of good cheer, take whatever might be given them and share it together as they always had? Captain was not a bad man. He was doing what his King wanted in taking them away. They understood that a king must be obeyed. And some day soon they would go home.

When the ship's boat carried them toward the stone quay in Plymouth Harbor, they were happy enough at the prospect of dry land to try singing as the sailors at the oars were doing.

The five Indians looked about them in the clear, early morning air. "Oh-ho," they said when they saw things which pleased them, sights such as the sun striking the glass eyes of the English houses and making them flash like mirrors. Before the day was done they had seen a great deal which puzzled them and did not please them. Silently they stored away questions to be asked when they should have the English words to do so.

Why did the English fasten their houses to the ground and fasten the houses to each other so that they could not be moved? What enemy did they fear that every one had his house walled and every wall was a-bristle with spikes? Why, if King James had so much wealth, did he allow some of his people to dress like kings but so many more to wear rags? Why did he allow his people to go hungry if he had grain and meat in his storehouses? Was it for a punishment that some must stand and ask for food and not be given it? Why were there misshapen people and sickly ones? Why did the English men hide their faces in hair and do the work of women?

No Indian would carry burdens on his back as the English did, not even a freshly shot deer when it was in danger of being devoured by wolves. No Indian would work in the fields or stitch clothing or bake bread as the Englishmen about them were doing. All this was the work of squaws. The work of men was hunting and fighting.

The five followed the Captain and Rosier through Plymouth's streets and along the hard cobblestones. They looked with swiftly darting eyes but with faces straight ahead. They marched as warriors.

On either side of the narrow streets people had gathered close-packed, near enough to touch them.

"Fancy, salvages," they heard the women say, and the bolder reply of the men, "Aye, wild men."

Almost at once the Indians had learned that there were more English in the world than there were leaves on the trees.

Straight on they marched toward what surely must be King James' house. It was built of stone and as high as a cliff, high enough for ravens to feel safe in nesting on its top. There were narrow slits in it with bars across. From some of the slits thrust the mouths of cannons, sakers and demi-culverins like those that spoke with the voice of thunder from the "Archangel."

Once they were inside the dark walls, the finest gentleman of all came forward to shake hands with Captain Waymouth. Then Nahanda, because he was a sagamore, advanced with his hand outstretched. He seized the fine gentleman's hand and pumped it up and down in the English fashion until he saw by the look on the other's face that he should stop.

"Welcome, King James, welcome," said Nahanada.

"I am not King James, but his servant, Sir Ferdinando Gorges, and at your service," said the Captain's friend with a bow.

A great deal of talk among the English followed. It was not like Indian talk, with one speaker continuing until he had spoken of everything that was

on his mind. It was chopped up like the talk of dogs
who barked together. The Indians could not hope to
follow it. They squatted on the cold stone floor, filled
up their pipe bowls, and struck fire from the imple-
ments in Assocomoit's leather bag. Soon their pipe
smoke curled toward the high ceiling and dimmed
the brightness of the weapons—swords, lances, pikes
and muskets—that filled the racks along the walls.

When the results of all this talk were made known
to them, they knew that they were to be separated,
and immediately.

Two of them were to go up to London to Sir John
Popham, the Lord Chief Justice, one of the backers
of Captain Waymouth's voyage. Three were to go
home with the fine gentleman, Sir Ferdinando
Gorges. He too, had joined with Lord Wardour in
sending out the "Archangel." He would take the men
home to his house in Plymouth. They would not live
here, because this was a fort of which he was commander.

Nahanada, the sagamore, would go to Sir John
Popham as a special mark of deference, and with
him would travel Assocomoit to be his servant. The
others would stay with Sir Ferdinando in Plymouth.

Nahanada's heart was heavy as they parted. He
was unhappy about this separation, but he was sad
for another reason as well. He knew now that he

would be away from his people at Pemaquid longer than he had first thought. He had hoped to be back with them again before their corn was gathered in, for harvest time was a dangerous one. It was then that the Tarrantines could be expected to sweep down on them. They would steal the corn the squaws had carefully cached in baskets and buried in deep pits. They would fire the rush-covered houses. They would kill the people, carry them off, or leave them to a hungry winter without corn. Nahanada knew that in the fall his people would need their sagamore more than ever. His good-bys to the others were sorrowful as he and Assocomoit were carried off to London.

Skitwarroes, Maneday, and Tisquantum were taken to Sir Ferdinando's house. After a few days Lady Gorges made a protest to her husband. "We must clothe these salvages," she said. "The servants gape so much at their nakedness that they get no work done. And they complain of being startled out of their wits by the creatures' sudden appearances with no clatter of proper boots to announce their coming. It is quite bad enough to have them about and leaving by the nearest window whenever they want out."

So a tailor was called in to measure the three for doublets and hose. A shoemaker was summoned to make boots for them. When the attire was ready, the Indians had to wear the leather and cloth prisons every day in spite of the July heat.

Gorges set a servant to teaching them more English. For a month or so this man was the center of attraction in the city. At the inn where he went for a sociable pint of ale he was surrounded by the curious and the admiring.

Were the wild men at Sir Ferdinando's kept in cages? Did they eat proper food, or raw meat? Wasn't he afraid of his charges? These were among the questions he was asked.

That the Indians were as civil and merry as any Christian, that they fed in a seemly fashion, neither eating nor drinking more than contented nature, their teacher had to admit. And there was never the least bit of discord among the three. It was share and share alike with them. He said such things so often that, after a time, his charges no longer held romantic or fearful attraction as a subject of conversation. In the town they became a part of everyday life. People spoke of them as "Sir Ferdinando's Indians" in a matter-of-fact way, just as his horses or dogs might be tagged with his name. After all, these weren't the first savages that the West Country of England had seen. Hadn't Sir Martin Frobisher, returning to Bristol in the "Gabriel," brought an Eskimo man, woman, and child from his voyage to seek Cathay? That had been in 1577, but there were still some who could remember the poor, dark-eyed babe who had lived but a short time. The man had sat for an artist both in his furred clothes and wearing English clothes, too, and the paint on the canvases was hardly dry before both the man and his wife were dead.

And several years after, in 1584, came Sir Walter Raleigh with two savages from Virginia. One of them had been carried back to his village on Croatoan Island by Sir Richard Grenville. Some remembered, too, a dead Indian displayed in London to holiday crowds for a penny a look.

We have no idea how Tisquantum, Skitwarroes, and Maneday managed to pass the time in Plymouth. All we know from the old accounts is that they learned some English and were finally able to answer Sir Ferdinando's questions about mines and fishing, the climate and plants, which tribes were friendly and which warring, in their native land.

Did Gorges allow his savages to hunt in the deer park of his country place? Were they able to use the skill they had acquired as small boys when it had been a matter of hitting a mark with their small arrows or going without breakfast? No one has written it down if they did, or whether they were forced to do "women's work" in spite of themselves.

Sir Ferdinando found his Indians most intelligent. He felt that Captain Waymouth had been justified in not leaving Owen Griffith behind in North Virginia. He learned enough from the trio to convince him that North Virginia, as New England was still called, was a good region to colonize and explore further even if he discovered no precious metals there.

He set about arousing interest in and gathering funds for another voyage to the New World. But times were very hard. It took long months, wearier even to the homesick Indians than to Gorges, to raise the sum that was needed. At last, in the summer of 1606, two vessels were ready to sail, one from Bristol and one from Plymouth.

Four of Waymouth's five Indians (no one has told us why Tisquantum remained behind) were divided between the two ships. Assocomoit and Maneday sailed on August 12, 1606, aboard the bark "Richard" from Plymouth. Captain Challons was master of this vessel. Later, in October of the same year, Nahanada and Skitwarroes said their good-bys to England at Bristol. Captain Pring was the master of their vessel.

The two captains had identical orders from their employers. Their instructions were to sail a route that was new to exploring voyagers from England. Instead of dropping south to the Azores, they were to follow a northerly course to Cape Breton and then turn south until they reached the home of their captives. This route was by no means a new one to English, French, and Portugese fishermen, however. They had been using it to get to their fishing grounds with perfect safety for more than a century. In 1580, the year that Sir Francis Drake returned home to great applause after his trip around the world in his "Golden Hind," more than three hundred fishing boats had sailed from European and English ports to work on the North American coasts. In fact, one old French fisherman had already made more than forty voyages to the fishing grounds by this "new" northerly route before 1609.

For this reason it is hard to imagine why Captain Challons so stubbornly refused to take that route as he was ordered. Was he perhaps terrified by the thought of getting caught in an ice pack?

His stubborness brought disaster to everyone—his backers, his crew, and the two poor Indians, Assocomoit and Maneday, who were unlucky enough to sail with him.

CHAPTER SEVEN

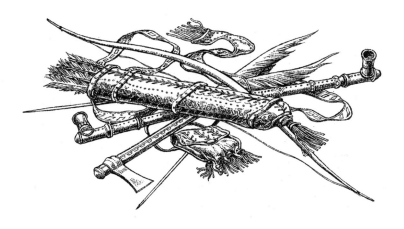

NAHANADA AND SKITWARROES were more fortunate than the other Indian pair; they were assigned to the vessel commanded by Captain Martin Pring. Although this ship's master was young, only twenty-six when he set out from Bristol in that summer of 1606, he had already served as captain of other vessels, the last of which had sailed to North Virginia. And most successful he had been in that recent command.

His had been one of the two vessels, the "Speedwell" and the "Discovery," that had visited Patuxet, Tisquantum's village, in 1603. Nor were his crew the first Europeans to have visited there. The fine harbor attracted explorers of that coast as surely as the North Pole does the magnetic needle. In the same year that Captain Waymouth was seizing his Indians farther north, Patuxet drew in Samuel Champlain, who was cruising the coast and looking for a suitable spot for a French colony. It drew in also Captain John Smith in 1614 after he had finished his Virginia adventures. The harbor attracted the most famous visitors of all in 1620—the Pilgrims. They finally established their settlement there and called Patuxet by its present name of Plymouth. And, strangely enough, one of the "Mayflower" sailors had visited there only the year before the colonists' arrival. In Governor Bradford's account of Plymouth Plantation he writes of this man having recommended Patuxet as the site for their colony.

The two vessels of Pring's 1603 voyage were searching not for a place to settle but for a cargo of sassafras. The root bark of the sassafras tree was steeped like tea and drunk as a remedy for all sorts of diseases. It was selling then in London for a good price, three shillings a pound, and was a fashionable remedy, the miracle drug of its time. Sassafras likes a sandy soil. Patuxet had that, so Pring's men found a fine supply of the root.

Now the men of the "Speedwell" and the "Discovery" were those about whom Tisquantum had told the Pemaquids. They were the Englishmen who had brought two great mastiffs, Toby and Trixie, to run down game to supply their masters with fresh meat. The dogs proved even more useful in frightening savages; the Indians had a mortal terror of the huge beasts.

Among Pring's men was a young sailor who owned a gitern. With this wire-stringed instrument, a good deal like a modern guitar, he made music that fascinated the Indians. Whenever he carried it ashore and strummed upon it, they flocked about him. They bribed him with presents of tobacco and pipes, of snakeskin belts and fawnskins, of anything and everything that they owned, to keep him playing. They formed a ring around him, twenty or more at a time, dancing and shouting, "Jo, ja, jo, ja, ja, jo," until the ground shook beneath their heavy tread and the player was too tired to go on.

Pring made the gathering of the sassafras root appear to be such attractive work that the savages joined in the task. He soon had both the "Speedwell" and the "Discovery" freighted with it. Perhaps the

Indians would not have worked so valiantly for their friend if they had realized that they were speeding the day of parting and of losing their music maker.

Yes, in spite of his youth, Pring was a veteran in experience with the savages when he sailed with Nahanada and Skitwarroes from Bristol. Now he hoped for even better success than he had had on the 1603 voyage. After all, he had now what he did not have before, a keen and intelligent Indian guide. The Captain carried out his employers' instructions to the letter. He sailed the northerly route without mishap, straight to the coast of Maine. Here at the rendezvous agreed upon, that small island-circled harbor used by Captain Waymouth, he waited for Captain Challons and the other vessel of the expedition, the "Richard."

At once Nahanada and Skitwarroes were reunited with their kinsmen. There was great rejoicing and feasting in the Pemaquid village. There was great happiness in Nahanada's heart to find that the Tarrantines had not destroyed his people.

Meanwhile, Captain Pring waited and waited for the "Richard." She had sailed some time ahead of his vessel and therefore should have been lying at anchor before his arrival. Pring questioned the Pemaquids. None admitted to having seen a winged ship at the anchorage. It was doubtful, then, that

the "Richard" had come and gone. Perhaps she had sprung a leak and put back to port. Perhaps she had been seized by pirates off the English coast; such marauders were getting more numerous and coming closer inshore every year.

Pring was troubled. The summer was over; cold winds were rattling dried brown oak leaves on the islands. If they were to make anything of this voyage before winter froze the coast, Pring knew that he must act at once and without Challons.

So he and his men ranged the shore. Pring observed the country and the Indians as they went, and he recorded what he saw. He gave this report to Sir Ferdinando when he returned home. Years after, when many others had explored along that same coast and mapped and charted it, Gorges wrote of Pring's report that it was "the most exact discovery of that coast that ever came to my hands since."

Pring's maps and charts gave a great impetus to colonizing plans for North Virginia. They aroused so much interest among the English that Gorges and Wardour and the others who had backed Waymouth in his kidnapping voyage felt that such an act had been justified. Without Nahanada's help, Pring's report would have been much less valuable.

The sagamore was rewarded for his services by being left to take up his old life once more. Poor Skitwarroes was less fortunate; for some reason he was taken back to England again. No one knows whether he went willingly or was bound and carried a prisoner as before.

And Nahanada, although happy at his good fortune, found that life would never again be the same for him. Now he knew that there were ambitious men across the sea, leaders in a country whose people were more numerous than the leaves on the trees. Any day they might appear on his native shores and drive out his people from their long-cultivated cornfields and the hunting lands which they burned over twice a year so that all might hunt and have food. Nahanada had seen the hedgerows and tightly walled small plots of land of England. He knew that over the seas land was cut up in small pieces and used only by its owners. He was sure that if the English came here they would chop up the land in the same way. They would never set fires in the spring and the fall and let them sweep freely over the countryside until rain quenched them. The land would become choked with brush and the game hard to get.

As far as Nahanada himself was concerned the English, by returning him, had proved themselves to be men of their word. But how long could all the

English be trusted? He could only wonder and wait and hope that the other four Pemaquids who had been carried off with him would have the same happy return.

CHAPTER EIGHT

NAHANADA AND ASSOCOMOIT had set out together
from Sir John Popham's London house, and when
they were parted to be taken to their separate ships,
farewells had scarcely seemed necessary. Although
Nahanada was sailing from Bristol and Assocomoit
from Plymouth, they were both sailing home. Surely
they would be together again soon.

They had left London in the same wagon, and
after Nahanada had changed into another for Bristol, Assocomoit, all alone, fell to thinking.

The heavy cart lumbered and lurched along the muddy road that was worn deep into the earth by the wheels and hoofs of many years. At times nothing was visible above the road's steep banks but the hedgerows lining it and a path of blue sky overhead.

The Indian recalled the London he was leaving and the land to which he was returning. He lay on his back and dreamed happily, half-asleep, of home. If he were less a savage he might have wondered which of the two countries was the more civilized.

The London he knew had its barbarous side. He thought of its stir and bustle, its houses black with soot, the Sunday bells snarling the air into a tangled skein of sound, the heads of executed criminals drying on pikes along London Bridge as a warning to others, the chained bears fighting for their lives against baiting dogs, and the thunder of applause from the theatres along the west bank of the Thames.

His thoughts turned toward home. He saw in his mind an Indian ball game, with both goals hung with the furs that would be the winners' trophies. He saw an Indian whale hunt so clearly that he could almost feel the rushing wind that came when the great mammal, with a bone-tipped harpoon planted in its side, drew the light birch canoe behind it with the speed of a bird in flight.

When he thought of Indian sport with a bear he

laughed aloud. His laughter so terrified the wagon driver that he gripped the handle of his whip and half-turned in his seat. He was fearful of being attacked by this wild man.

Assocomoit scarcely noticed the driver's actions. His mind was far away in strawberry time on the shores at home. It was there, when the berries were ripe, that they sometimes saw a great bear swimming to one of the islands in his eagerness to get the fruit growing upon it. The men who were near often plunged into the water and swam after him. When they had overtaken the creature they struggled with him in the water until one of them was able to get astride the furry back. Here he would stick, with his sides and perhaps his face scratched and bleeding from the thrusts of the animal's claws, until the bear swam himself into a state of exhaustion. Then his rider could easily knife him.

With these thoughts Assocomoit passed the time until the wagon lurched into Plymouth. Here he met Maneday, whom he scarcely recognized at first in his English clothes and clumping boots, although he himself was similarly disguised.

Together they sailed aboard the "Richard."

No sooner did Captain Henry Challons have the "Richard" on the high seas than he proceeded to disobey his employers. Off he sailed, south by way of the

Azores as he had always done, to make for the West
Indies and thence to North Virginia. Perhaps he reasoned that by the time he reached port after a successful voyage his employers would have forgotten
their stupid instructions for him to take the northerly
route.

Whatever unknown dangers he hoped to avoid
by sailing south, he ran head on into most of the
perils in the mariner's book. First they were caught
in a terrific storm off Madeira in the Canary Islands.
Later they ran into a calm: fourteen torrid days of
no wind and no progress. The merciless sun beat
down on them and with its heat came sickness, always made worse aboard ship in those days by the
sailors' inadequate diet.

Finally, by the time they made the West Indies,
Captain Challons was a very sick man, so sick that
he decided to cruise among the Caribbean Islands
until he recovered. He seemed to have forgotten not
only that he had a rendezvous with Captain Pring
but that here, in Spanish waters and among Spanish
isles, was no place for an Englishman who valued his
life. Two years before, James I of England had ended
the long war between England and Spain. Although
there was peace officially, the Spanish would not tol-
erate English vessels so near the route of their treasure fleet.

In the West Indies, Captain Challons' men replaced the ropy water in the "Richard's" casks with a fresh supply. They sailed luxuriously and aimlessly among the mountainous green islands, enjoying exotic fruits and vegetables and a variety of the fish so easily caught in these clear waters. They marveled to see fireflies along the shore at night, seeming as bright as the tropical stars.

It was now almost three months since they had left Plymouth. Assocomoit and Maneday must have begun to wonder whether they would ever see home again. Soon, however, something happened that made home farther away than before.

John Stoneman, the pilot on the "Richard," had also been pilot on the "Archangel." He and the two Indians knew each other well. It was Stoneman who wrote down the story of the voyage of the "Richard" and its disastrous end.

It all began, he said, as they sailed past the island of Dominica. Some one of the "Richard's" crew spied a white flag among the palm trees fringing the shore. He sang out. The captain agreed with the rest that the flag might be the signal of some European in distress. They "remembered the Golden Rule" and "stayed a little." Soon they were amazed to see a canoe under sail, the first canvas they had ever seen on a native dugout. The craft was making for them.

As it neared, a pleading voice called out across the water. At first none of them could understand it but after a time some scholar aboard, perhaps the captain, perhaps Stoneman himself, recognized the speech as Latin and translated for the rest.

"I beseech you, as you are Christians, for Christ's sake, show some mercy and compassion to me," the voice entreated. "I am a preacher of the word of God, a friar of the Order of Franciscans in Seville, by name of Friar Blasius."

By the time their scholar had translated the beseeching words the crew was lining the "Richard's" rail and looking down into the dugout. The canoe was piled with island fruits, bananas and plantains and cassava roots, and manned by ferocious, scowling natives. The friar, sumburned and bearded, held the tiller.

Captain Challons, or perhaps the scholar speaking for him, asked, "What are you doing here?"

"For sixteen months I have been a slave to the savages. Two other friars of my company they murdered and threw into the sea," said the monk.

"How," asked Captain Challons, "did you get so much favor to preserve *your* life, your brethren being murdered?"

"Because I did teach the savages how to fit them sails to their canoes, and so to ease them of much labor in rowing, which greatly pleased them," answered the friar.

The Captain was still not quite ready to believe their visitor. After all, this man was a Spaniard and therefore the last person for an Englishman to trust. "Where did you get linen cloth to make those sails?" he asked.

"Two years ago three galleons to the West Indies were cast away on the island of Guadalupa, where abundance of linen cloth and other merchandise was cast on shore," he said.

"How came you to be here?" asked the Captain.

"Every year the King of Spain doth send out of every monastery certain friars into the remote parts of the Indies, both to seek to convert Indians and to seek out what benefits or commodities might be had in those parts, and what force the savages were of."

At last his answers quieted the Captain's suspicions. Spaniard or not, his distress should be relieved. There was no one aboard the "Richard" who did not feel pity for the man. The Captain invited the friar aboard. He answered the natives' protests at the friar's leaving with musket shot. This language they understood better than Latin. In a panic they paddled off without remembering to use their valued sail.

Captain Challons offered to set the friar ashore

on one of the islands where he would find other
countrymen, and he turned the "Richard" towards
Puerto Rico. He must have known that he was going where he had no right to risk his ship. He was
putting his head into the mouth of the Spanish lion
but he sailed on, full of the pleasure that comes from
doing a good deed. They left Friar Blasius on a lonely
shore in the care of two Spanish herdsmen and sailed
away with a gift of fresh meat from the herders.

Their pleasure in these gifts and their own kindness was short-lived. Another storm soon buffeted
them. Rain lashed them; wind harried them. Then
early one November morning they made out through
an engulfing fog another vessel, then another, one
here, one there, until they saw eight. And carved on
the transom of one they saw a sight that chilled even
the dullest of the crewmen. There, all red and gold
and blue, were the arms of the royal house of Castile. They were in the midst of a Spanish fleet.

And no ordinary Spanish fleet, either, but, as it
turned out, the twice-yearly convoy which carried
New World treasure to Seville in Spain. Now in these
jealously guarded waters any Spanish vessel would
be a fidgety neighbor to have, but a fleet laden with,
gold and silver ingots was the most dangerous of all.

Soon a shot whistled through the "Richard's" rigging. Her mainsail fell in shreds on her deck. Two of

the Spanish vessels sailed near and demanded that the English speak with their admiral. The Captain had no choice but to obey; his crew was outnumbered, and his mainsail was useless. Captain Challons ordered the "Richard's" colors hauled down as a signal of surrender.

A boat crowded with armed men put out at once from the Spanish flagship. The warlike gang sprang aboard the English ship. It was apparent at once that the conversation their admiral wanted was with their swords, rapiers, and half-pikes.

They drove the "Richard's" crew below decks with fierce thrusts of their weapons. Captain Challons was badly wounded. As for poor Assocomoit, a sword pierced his arm. In terror he tried to hide under a locker. The Spaniards found him and thrust at him. Over and over he cried out in protest, "King James his ship! King James his ship!"

When the invaders had the whole ship's company below decks and disarmed, they drove them up again. They forced them at swords' point to leap down into their ship's boat. Then they rowed them to the Spanish flagship. On the passage the English looked back and saw that the Spanish who remained behind were plundering their vessel of its supplies.

Once aboard the flagship, Captain Challons got nowhere in his protests to his captors. He showed them King James' commission as legal proof of their business on this side of the world. The Admiral refused to read the document. The Captain told them that the "Richard" was in these waters to return to his countrymen a Spanish friar that they had rescued from the natives. The Admiral couldn't have been less interested. He had nothing to say except that the crew and company of the "Richard" were to be divided among the ships of his fleet and carried to Spain.

There was no Englishman in the "Richard's" crew who had not been brought up on tales of Spanish cruelty. All during the years of the Spanish wars the dread of invasion had hung over England. To these men of the "Richard" the bogeyman had always been a Spaniard.

They were soon to learn that the childhood tales had a basis in fact.

CHAPTER NINE

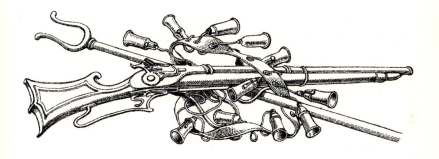

THE "RICHARD" WAS captured by the Spanish treasure fleet three months sailing from Plymouth. Not until Christmas Eve, almost a month and a half later, did the first storm-battered vessel of the treasure fleet, with its English and Indian captives, limp up to the bar across the mouth of the Quadalquivir River in Spain. Winter storms had driven her off her course and her pilot had proved incompetent. In fact, if the worried Spaniards hadn't forced John Stoneman to act in his place, they would never have made port at all.

John Stoneman and the other English on this first
vessel were carried some miles upriver to Seville and
clapped into prison. Here they were joined by their
former shipmates as one vessel and then another
safely made harbor at San Lucar. A month had
passed since the day Stoneman was thrown into
prison, and still Captain Challons and the two Indians
had not been thrust in among them. The English
prisoners gave them up as lost. After all, they had
been wounded when the Spanish boarded the "Richard." They might well have died at sea of their
wounds.

But finally the last vessel of the Spanish fleet made
San Lucar. Here, at the bar, the captives were
moved, as the rest had been, to a shallow-draught
boat. Along with part of the treasure from the Indies
—gold and silver ingots, packets of pearls, emeralds
and spices—they were swept upriver. Soon the city of
Seville gleamed before their dazzled eyes, its white-
washed stucco cubes of houses turned the golden
color of honey by the sunlight.

Although the Spaniards had driven the Moors
from this city more than four hundred years before,
it still looked a Moorish city. The great square tower
of the Giralda, from which Moslem muezzins had
once called the faithful to prayer, thrust its way up
through closely packed houses. The Moorish bridge

to Triana still floated on the river, rising and falling with the tide. The Moorish Tower of Gold rose from the river bank not far from the spot where the Captain, Assocomoit, and Maneday, heavy with chains, were taken ashore.

After that day, Assocomoit and Maneday did not see the warm sunshine again for many months.

Once ashore in Seville, Captain Challons pulled out the roll of parchment that was King James' commission for the voyage and thrust it into the face of every Spaniard who asked him questions.

"Here is legal proof of our business in the New World," he would say. "Why do you hold us? England and Spain are at peace. You can have no reason to consider us as enemies."

Neither the truth in his words nor the magic supposed to lie in the black figures written on the roll gained them their freedom. They were marched to a building not far from the great square tower of the Giralda. On its doorstep Captain Challons stood his ground.

"I refuse to enter," he said, "I am a subject of His Majesty, King James of England."

Assocomoit and Maneday echoed him. "King James, his man," they both said.

Then all three felt the weight of the guards' iron

clubs on their backs. They stumbled into the darkness beyond the open door. Behind them they heard the door slammed shut; then the bolts were shot and the chains were fastened.

The prison was like a cave, cold and gray. Its stench assaulted their noses. Its rottenness choked their throats.

"Den of animals!" growled the Captain and clapped his dingy handkerchief over his nose and mouth. The Indians held their breaths as long as they could.

Before their eyes had adjusted to the darkness, their ears caught a murmur that moved through the place like the stirring of an unhappy wind. It was the sound of men in pain and despair.

Two more guards joined those who had driven the newcomers inside the door. These had shaved heads and wore leg irons, but although they themselves were prisoners their blows were no lighter than the others'. They drove the Captain and the two Indians down a short flight of stone steps into the great main room of the prison.

"Dogs of English, sots, drunkards," they shouted with each blow.

The Captain and the Indians shuffled through knee-deep straw as they were driven along. It wasn't

until each had been shackled to one of the great iron rings set in the stone walls of the room and the guards had left that they dared to look around for familiar faces.

When they saw the men from the "Richard," they found them changed beyond belief. Their shipmates were gaunt and haggard, and most wore a look of dull despair.

Captain Challons called out softly and fearfully to them. "Good day to you, lads. How does it fare with you?"

"An evil day, Captain, not a good one, is that which brings you here to this foul place. We are well-nigh starved," answered one.

"Aye," groaned another, "starved, and in our weakened state we fall sick. Poor old Robert Cooke is already at death's door with the flux."

A shriek rang out from a dim corner and echoed through the room.

" 'Tis Mr. St. John, sir," said one of the sailors, "he's down with a calenture. It breeds queer fancies in him. He thinks often that he is back among the green fields of home. Wait but a moment and he will try to stand and throw himself down upon the turf."

Soon, as the sailor had predicted, there came a sound from St. John that was half-groan, half-cry. He struggled to rise in his shackles. The chains jerked him back when he had reached the end of their short length. He fell on his side, and once more his cries rang out.

Suddenly a crop-haired guard with but one eye came into the room. Although he wore leg irons he moved with surprising rapidity until he stood over the delirious St. John.

"Lutheran, be still!" he roared. Then he raised a club and brought it down upon the sick man and beat him until he no longer made any sound.

The helpless prisoners covered their eyes or watched in horror. A great roar of curses came from those not too stupefied by their own troubles to protest.

The guard went to the center of the room and stood gripping his club and threatening to lunge at the next offender.

The room became silent and he left.

When he had gone, the bosun of the "Richard" spoke to Captain Challons from between clenched teeth. "Watch out for that one," he growled, "he's a mad fiend straight from Hell. Had I but one wish to last for the rest of my life I would ask only to meet him man to man in an honest fight. I'd tear him limb from limb and take the consequences with pleasure. Pass on the word to the two savages that One Eye is the worst of the lot."

No food came to the prisoners until the next midday, and then the meal was soup and bread. The soup earned that name only because it was liquid, while the bread was like a stone. Even when it was sopped in soup the men could scarcely chew it. Most of them had scurvy, so that their loosened teeth ached continually.

Soon after the meal the prison warden approached the Captain.

"Buenas días," he said. "Ah, my captain, you want more better food for your friends, *no es verdad?* That we will do for *dinero.*" He opened his palm and pointed to the coins lying in it. *"Dinero.* You come. I show you how to get it."

He freed the Captain from his iron ring and led him off.

At the end of the day the Captain returned, blinking at the dimness, dingy handkerchief to his nose. After the guard had secured him to his ring and then gone away, Challons spoke. His voice was that of a man completely shattered.

"This is no ordinary prison. It may be that we will never leave it alive. It belongs to the Casa de Conratación, the bureau that controls all the affairs of the Indies, every detail of them. Since we were taken among the islands of the Indies we are theirs, no matter that England and Spain are not at war. They can starve us, hang us, or burn us, or let us go free, the which last they show little likelihood of doing."

"How can this be?" asked John Stoneman.

The Captain went on in a spiritless sing-song to repeat the horrible lesson he had recently learned. "The gentlemen who run this Casa are accountable only to the House of Castile because Columbus, exploring for Her Majesty Queen Isabella of Castile, won the Indies for her and her kingdom alone. 'Tis all hers, the Indies and their wealth, and the Kingdom of Spain has no power over it nor over the Casa which runs the Indies for her. And we are at their mercy."

There was silence for a time while the men of the "Richard" faced the hard facts.

Then Stoneman remembered the Captain's errand. "What of the money, Captain? Were you able to secure some to better our fare?"

"Aye, but at usurious rates. Two of our countrymen now resident in Seville will loan it, but, because they see little chance of its return, their rates must be great. The robber who runs this prison will take the greater part of it for our food, since my English friends tell me that two shillings will not buy in Spain what one will in England. And how does Mr. St. John?"

This was a needless question. Like the rest, Challons could not help but hear the sick man's delirious talk, full of laughter and groans. He remembered, but he did not tell the others, the chilling news that the burial of their dead would cost them more than to feed their living.

As the weeks passed Captain Challons left the prison daily. By paying a large sum of money he was allowed to come and go. This was called being in "open" prison. The two Indians watched him go off with dull eyes. None of the sunshine from the outside returned with him—only terrifying rumors.

The committee that ruled the Casa questioned and cross-questioned Challons. They wanted to know all he knew, and more, too, about North Virginia. Scuttling back and forth like a frightened beetle to these sessions, Captain Challons picked up many unpleasant reports. The Count of Lemos had announced that he would hang all the "Richard's" crew himself if need be. The "Richard" had been sunk in the river. If the English had not been forgotten by their friends at home, they would have been freed long before. And so on. Until the day when Captain Challons was forbidden on the pain of a beating and a fine of three hundred ducats to talk with Assocomoit and Maneday.

The two Indians had grown too listless to eat. Although they had been hardened all their lives, from the moment when their mothers had tumbled them as babies into a snowbank, nothing they had learned or suffered had taught them to withstand imprisonment. Hunger and lack of sleep, cold and torture they could endure, but not this loss of freedom. No Indian had ever shut away another from light and air, the open sky and the sweep of the seasons. Confinement was slow death to both Assocomoit and Maneday.

They envied Nathaniel Humfries, the bosun, who met with a quicker death.

One day the brutal, one-eyed guard had been abusing the prisoner who lay next to Humfries. This so enraged the bosun that, quick as a flash, he stretched his chains to the utmost and got one foot under the guard's leg shackles. The Spaniard tripped and fell forward.

He rose with a roar. He lunged at the bosun with a drawn knife and drove it to the hilt in the bosun's belly.

Humfries lay bleeding and unattended. Soon prison fever set in, and within a few days he was dead. The guards tied a rope to his ankles and dragged his body past all the "Richard's" crew on its way to burial.

During these miserable, nightmarelike days, Captain Challons was writing letters and sending them to England. Although no help reached the prisoners, it is known that the letters of appeal were delivered in England. One that he wrote in June, 1607, to King James' chief minister, Lord Cecil, is still among the state papers of England. Full of entreaties for help before it is too late, the letter ends with the bad news that Challons' two Indians had been taken from him as slaves.

Lord Cecil was not unmoved by the sufferings that the Captain described. He was concerned, and so were others in high places; but they could do nothing. Their royal master, King James, forgetful of how the English hated the Spanish, was trying to arrange a marriage between his son and a princess of Spain. He wanted no unpleasantness between the two countries while his son was visiting in Spain. His subjects were allowed to suffer on in prison.

And because the committee of the Casa, not content with the staggering wealth that was pouring in from the Indies, wanted more, they were not likely to release the English. They wanted to pry from them all the possible information about the resources of North Virginia and England's plans for colonies there.

The men of the Casa knew that John Stoneman had been in that country. They allowed him, too, to buy "open prison." Daily he went out for questioning.

They tried to bribe him to work for them, but failed. Then Stoneman picked up a rumor in the streets that he was to be put to the torture. He was to be placed on the rack to tell what more he knew about English plans and to tell whether Challons hadn't been on the way, with the Indians as his guides, to found a colony in the Spanish Indies.

This prospect was too much for Stoneman. He fled from Seville, forfeiting his bail. Eventually he reached England, but his going placed the prisoners left behind in greater danger than before.

The months dragged on into a year and more.

Then one day a horseman galloped up to Lord Cecil's London headquarters with a letter from Sir Ferdinando Gorges at Plymouth. Among other news in it there was word of Captain Challons: "Captayne Challones hath made an escape out of Spayne and is arrived here—which he hath done for that he saw his cause so desperate—But poore gentleman, his wants are soe great now—as he hath no meanes to supplie his present necessities."

So did Gorges forgive the weak, disobedient captain for the loss of so much time, the vessel, and the two Indians.

Of the crewmen left languishing at Seville there was no word then or later. Of Maneday, who suffered so much through the captain's disobedience, we hear no more. He must have lived out his life so far from home as a Spanish slave. He may have been chained to the rowers' bench in a galley or forced to labor in a mine. He may have served a private master or escaped from slavery and wandered through the streets of Seville, lost forever in the ragged army of beggars.

We hear about Assocomoit later. By hook or crook, he escaped from slavery and got himself from Spain to England. But none of the accounts tell how he made this amazing trip. They ignore him until once more he came to Plymouth and stood on Sir Ferdinando's doorstep asking for food and protection.

CHAPTER TEN

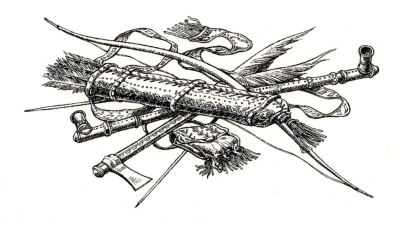

Sir Ferdinando Gorges was a man in whom hope died hard. Skitwarroes had found that out. The Indian was in the Gorges household while the bad news trickled back from Challons in the Seville prison. All during this time Sir Ferdinando was working on plans for another expedition to New England.

Skitwarroes had come back to England with Pring after Nahanada had been left with the Pemaquids. Pring had delivered him at Plymouth on the same day that he had delivered his report. Skitwarroes had seen Gorges' face light up as he studied its pages. The excitement and hope that the report roused in him sustained him all through the discouraging news from Seville.

Then, one morning in the early spring of 1607, Gorges called Skitwarroes to him and introduced him to a stranger.

"Here is your new master, Raleigh Gilbert," he said. "You will go with him and be his guide to your native country. In June of this year, if all goes well, he and Master George Popham will set sail from this harbor with two vessels, to proceed in company to North Virginia. You will take your orders from him, and when your time of service is done you shall be free as the wind forever."

Skitwarroes grunted in assent. He had heard this sort of talk before. He knew that he would be free only when he was free. While the two Englishmen talked he listened and studied the man Gilbert. He had by this time seen many hearty young Englishmen. Raleigh Gilbert was perhaps the heartiest of them all.

He had clapped Skitwarroes on the back by way of greeting. Now he paced the room like a caged animal and kept breaking in on Gorges' talk. More and more the Indian found himself setting his jaw and his mind against Gilbert.

Skitwarroes learned that the young Englishman

was not the first of his family to be attracted by the thought of the New World. His father, Sir Humphrey Gilbert, had been drowned on the way home from a disastrous expedition to Newfoundland. His uncle was Sir Walter Raleigh, who had sailed to America for Elizabeth, the Queen, and who had been clapped into the Tower of London three years ago by King James. Even from prison he was urging Englishmen to go overseas.

Skitwarroes also learned that Gilbert and Popham were planning more than a visit to his native shores. They were planning to stay.

Gorges rubbed his hands in pleasure at the thought. "Ah, Raleigh, my friend, this time we shall do it, I expect. Now we've got fellows of the right sort, fully determined to remain in the country. They're not the lily-livered sort that have set forth before, with a full mind to remain till there's talk of the homeward passage, then home they come, tails between legs. And what is more, this time we've got men of every trade—tinker, tailor, and candle-stickmaker, so to speak. Not to mention ship's carpenters. We plan to set these last to work at once, hewing out timbers for building a bark which perhaps will pay a goodly share of our costs."

Raleigh was on his feet at this. "With great oaks

upon the shore, what's to prevent our building a fleet?"

Here Skitwarroes left the room. He was of two minds. One was to hold back whatever he knew from this Gilbert. The other was do anything—even to helping Gilbert—in order to speed himself upon the homeward way.

Soon the colonists began to assemble in Plymouth. Skitwarroes met Master Popham, an old man who moved heavily. The Indian thought that he and Raleigh Gilbert differed from each other as much as any two Englishmen he had met.

Popham was to command the vessel called the "Gift of God"; Gilbert was master of the other, "The Mary and John." Skitwarroes would voyage with the latter. The two vessels sailed in June of 1607. Friends and relatives flocked to town to say farewell to the colonists, whom they might never see again. Skitwarroes' heart danced to the music of the flutes and oboes on the dock. He was ready to burst with pleasure when at last the "Mary and John's" sails filled and the cannon thundered a good-by from Sir Ferdinando's fort.

Both ships touched at Flores in the Azores for supplies. Skitwarroes went with the sailors who rowed the "Mary's" longboat ashore for fresh water.

At the well the English had to wait while sailors who spoke another tongue drew their water. These dawdled at their task until one of the "Mary's" sailors called out, "Do not hurry, Froggies. We have all day to wait."

The answer, although he did not understand its words, was plain in meaning to Skitwarroes and the whole company of English. It was an insult of the sort that must be answered with doubled fists. The "Mary's" sailors sprang upon the others and soon all the water-drawers were rolling upon the ground. If Raleigh Gilbert hadn't appeared with his sword drawn, the fight might have gone on for a long time.

He called off his men and the work of watering went on. Soon both the "Gift of God" and the "Mary and John" were ready for sea again. The "Gift's" sails were broken out and up came her anchor. Aboard the "Mary," too, preparations were almost as far along when Skitwarroes gave a shout. He had spotted something the others had been too busy to notice. A longboat had put out from one of the ships anchored in the harbor. It made for the "Mary" and pulled alongside. Almost before Skitwarroes' warning had died away, the rowers were swarming over the English vessel's side. They brandished swords and clubs as they hit the deck.

"King James, his ship!" shouted Skitwarroes in protest.

The fight that had begun at the well was being continued on the "Mary's" deck. Gilbert ordered the distress signal run up to call back the "Gift' to their aid. Not once, however, did the men of their consort ship look back, and things were going badly for the "Mary's" men as the distance between the two vessels widened.

At last the crew of a neighboring English ship came to their rescue and parted the fighters. The "Mary" was able to stand out to sea. Already the "Gift's" sails were small in the distance and soon they dropped below the horizon. The voyage that was to have been made in company became a lonely duel with wind and waves.

Days became weeks, but at long last Skitwarroes saw with his keen savage's eyes the round blue hills on the mainland which the sailors took for clouds. Before many hours the dark-green mass of the shores became saw-toothed ranks of fir trees. A group of headlands separated into a cluster of islands and opened up to show the spars of their consort, the "Gift," at anchor in Captain Waymouth's old harbor. How happy the crews and colonists of both ships were at this joyful meeting!

Raleigh boomed his thanks for skillful piloting, and Skitwarroes thought that this might be the moment to request a visit with his people. He wanted to meet Nahanada and talk over with him what should be done about these English who proposed to stay in their country.

It was then almost midnight. To Skitwarroes' surprise and displeasure Raleigh said, "Let us man the longboat and go to your village at once. We must get about our business here. Time's a-wasting. Let us find a place for President Popham's colony. Then Admiral Gilbert can be free to explore along the coast. We'll go at once."

He clapped a hearty hand on Skitwarroes' shoulder. The Indian felt anger rising in him, but he could only assent to going. Perhaps he could somehow outwit Gilbert and have some words with Nahanada before the English met him.

He guided Gilbert's men to a harbor on the western side of the bay. From here it was a short march across a point of land to the Pemaquids' village. As the longboat nosed into the harbor, Skitwarroes offered to go ashore alone and carry out Gilbert's business with his people. Gilbert refused his offer.

They landed, and left two men to guard the longboat. The rest set out after the Indian on the trail to the Pemaquid village. By this time the sky was paling into dawn, but Skitwarroes knew his way so well that he could have led them in the dark up across the humpback of this point. He had often rehearsed it in his mind during the long months away, every step of the trail, from great oak to moss-dripping spruce, from boulder to lichened ledge.

They marched for several miles. Then Skitwarroes stopped short. He would not lead these people to his village. He would not have them settling there and driving the Pemaquids from their cornfields. Shaking his head, he turned to Gilbert, who was close at his heels.

"My people are gone, all are gone away," he said. "Let us go back to the boat."

Gilbert answered him angrily. "Do not trick us, Skitwarroes. We will not turn back until such time as we have spoken with some of your people."

Skitwarroes knew that he had no choice; he had to lead on.

Soon he saw his village near the curve of white sands where the Pemaquid River meets the sea. Smoke rose from the holes in the woven rush roofs. Canoes were drawn up on the shore. Across the hard open ground about which the houses clustered small children padded. Everything was just as it always had been. Near at hand grew the corn, the grain which he had not seen in England. Already its stalks had tasseled out and the silk stirred slightly above the ears. The sound of the rustling leaves brought a sudden homesickness with it, sharper even than any Skitwarroes had felt in England.

Then the dogs caught the strangers' scent and howled. At once their alarms brought together a group of braves whose shouts drowned out the barking of the curs. Skitwarroes knew from this response that his people were on the alert against an enemy. He stood his ground and called out across the distance between them, "I am Skitwarroes, come back again."

The warriors laid aside the bows they had picked up and came on. Nahanada was the first to reach his cousin and embrace him. Then, remembering English manners, he shook Raleigh Gilbert's hand. Soon all the warriors and the English were shaking hands.

They moved on into the village. Skitwarroes saw his young wife standing among the women. He longed to hear her voice, which would be softer than any woman's he had heard in England, but he waited to speak to her until the men should finish their talk. He knew that she, too, would now bide her time as patiently as she had during his two years away.

For two hours the English stayed with the Pemaquids. They visited among the rush houses and sampled whatever was cooking in the brass and earthen pots hanging inside over the fires.

In the meantime Nahanada and his cousin talked earnestly together. The news the sagamore had to tell was grave. Their dreaded enemies to the north, the Tarrantines, were making war on Bashaba and all his allies, among them Sasanoa, the overlord among the tribes around the Pemaquids. He had called upon the men of this village for help. Nahanada insisted that Skitwarroes leave the English at once and join with them.

Skitwarroes was troubled. He was afraid of what the English might do, both to himself and to his people, if he broke his promise to them. They expected his help in finding a fit place to fasten their houses and in establishing trade among his own people. Skitwarroes told the sagamore that tomorrow he would bring the English back again for trading. Then he would tell his cousin whether or not he would join him against the Tarrantines. Nahanada understood his problems; after all, he knew the English.

The party went back along the trail to their boat and then eastward across the bay to where the two vessels lay. But the next day—that on which Skitwarroes had promised Nahanada to come again—was Sunday. The English followed their custom, and not

even Gilbert would march or work. They would not
allow Skitwarroes to leave them, either. He had to
wait for Monday to set out once more for the Pemaquids.

This time the party went all the way by water.
They sailed out around the point and into the bay of
the Pemaquids. Some of the men were with Gilbert
in the longboat, others with Captain Popham in the
shallop.

As the boats made in toward the village, Nahanada and his men waded out into the surf to meet
them. Angrily the sagamore ordered the English not
to land.

The English looked as surprised and hurt as children do when a playmate refuses to go on with yesterday's game. Skitwarroes knew why the sagamore
was so forbidding. Nahanada had troubles enough
getting ready to march with his warriors to Sasanoa
without having fifty Englishmen come among his
people.

Skitwarroes knew, too, that if the English wanted
to land, land they would. Even if they were told why
they were not wanted, they would pay no attention.
To them, the affairs of the Indians were of no more
importance than those of ants whose hill they might
stir up with a stick. They might notice either ants

or Indians busy at work or at war, but they would not trouble to understand their doings.

As Skitwarroes expected, the two leaders ordered their men to land. Once ashore, they proposed that Nahanada trade with them. Now it was Skitwarroes' turn to be surprised, for Nahanada agreed. Skitwarroes did not know that word had come from Bashaba by way of Sasanoa that above all things he wanted white's men's guns for his war with the Tarrantines. If Nahanada saw a chance to get muskets, he must seize it.

When the sagamore held out for guns instead of the usual trading articles, Popham and Gilbert both refused to part with a single firearm.

Nahanada became very angry and called out a sharp order to his people. Suddenly papooses propped in their cradle boards against house frames were picked up and slung on their mothers' backs, walking children were herded ahead, dogs were led off on leather thong leashes. Skitwarroes stopped only long enough to tell the English that he would rejoin them the next day and then he, too, followed the rest. He looked back once before the trees hid the English from sight. He saw them standing and staring at the village that had been so suddenly and wordlessly deserted. They looked hurt and angry. Then the English shrugged their shoulders as if to say "You can't do business with people who are not here," and then they waded out to their boats.

When the Pemaquids were sure that the English were gone for good they came back. They took down the rush mats from their house frames, rolled them and made ready for the trail. They were off to join Sasanoa.

CHAPTER ELEVEN

IN SPITE OF SKITWARROES' hasty promise to return
to Gilbert and Popham and help them get established, he did not see the colonists the next day nor
for many days afterward. He had decided to help
his own people. He was glad that he had come in time
to aid them against their enemies.

He tried to forget the English at once. He took off
his heavy shoes and gratefully put on the soft deerskin moccasins that his wife had made for him. Now
he could move as silently as the other Indians. He

took off his woolen doublet and hose and would have thrown them into the fire but for his wife. She begged for them to use to soften the cradle board. She hoped now for a papoose. He blotted from his mind all memory of his captivity, and only occasionally was he reminded of the men who had carried him off.

Twice a group of warriors coming to join Sasanoa reported seeing the bearded strangers. Some said that they had called out as the Indians had paddled past their great canoes and had invited them to trade, but the Indians had not stopped. Others reported that the English had moved these winged canoes into the narrow mouth of the Kennebec River near a spit of land. Already they were at work, felling trees and making a great house upon that low-lying land.

Soon afterward the Tarrantines swept down upon Sasanoa and his allies. Before they withdrew, Sasanoa's son lay dead from a Tarrantine musket bullet.

Sasanoa called Nahanada and his cousin to him. They knew the English; they must go to them and persuade them to exchange guns for furs. The Tarrantines would stay away for a time, it was hoped; when they came back Sasanoa wanted to meet them with gunfire.

Both Pemaquids were reluctant to make this visit; they well knew that the English did not want to give

up their guns, and they were afraid of being seized
again. However, Sasanoa's orders were to be obeyed.
They returned home to get their kinsmen to go to the
English with them.

They found some of the squaws placing the last of
the corn harvest in baskets, while others dug pits.
With their clam-shell hoes the women dragged back
the soil from the openings that they had dug, then,
when the baskets were in place, they pushed back the
loose earth to cover them. They smoothed the ground
over the caches and covered them with leaves. Then
Skitwarroes and several of the men felled small oak
trees that stood near the pits so that their brush and
winter-clinging foliage could hide the spot. The Tarrantines must not find the crop. The Pemaquids were
going to need it; all signs pointed to a hard, cold
winter. Winter berries were heavy upon the shrubs
and the chattering squirrels had never worn coats
so thick.

The whole village, with all their possessions, took
to the water. The next morning their nine canoes
swept into the Kennebec. They saw at once that the
English had already made a wooden wall upon the
spit of land. The black mouth of a cannon jutted
through it.

The sagamore Nahanada and Skitwarroes went
ashore at once to carry out the dreaded errand.

The English were noisily at work within the wall, building a great house. As the Indians appeared, they threw down their tools—hammers and saws and broad axes for hewing timbers—and greeted them. Gilbert clapped Skitwarroes on the back just as if he had not broken his promise to return. Master Popham wheezed a stately greeting. He looked more tired and worried than the Indian had remembered him. However, he urged all the Pemaquids to stay for a feast.

When they sat down to a meal of fish and pease porridge, venison and partridge, all washed down with strong water, the Indians told the English the news. They described the large-scale war that was going on along the coast. But even when the talk turned to trading, they did not mention their desire for English guns. They sent their squaws down to the canoes to bring up their best trading pelts.

Gilbert and Popham brought out their bags of trading goods and displayed their bright mirrors and tinkling bells and brilliant feathers. To make good feeling, Nahanada allowed the exchange of a few furs for the English goods. Skitwarroes was glad that he had done so when he saw the look of pleasure on his wife's face as he tossed her a mirror and a bell.

Then it was time to try for guns. Both Gilbert and Popham stiffened at the mention of muskets.

"But what need have *you* of our guns, my friends?" asked Gilbert. "You could scarce catch a bird on the wing or a leaping doe with the ease with which now you do with your excellent and most deadly arrows. As for muskets, they are treacherous machines at best. Keep clear of them."

Nahanada abruptly ordered the pelts carried back to the canoes. Guns were what he wanted and nothing else. He declared the trading ended.

Then the sagamore had a sudden thought. He turned and spoke softly of it to Skitwarroes.

"If we could lead them to Bashaba, he of all men could persuade them to part with their guns," he said.

Skitwarroes agreed, and Nahanada made an offer to pilot the English to the great overlord Bashaba, from whom they could get the finest furs of all.

Gilbert's face lit up. He was pleased to have a chance to meet Bashaba and to explore the coast between the Penobscot River, where Bashaba now was, and the Kennebec. When he said as much, Master Popham urged him not to take any of the men away and interrupt the work on the fort and the dwelling house.

Nahanada said that he could arrange the trip only if it were made at once. Gilbert, ignoring Master

Popham, made plans to go to the Pemaquids' village in two days' time.

Now the sun was sliding low in the west. Some of the Pemaquids, heavy with food and drink, were paddling across the river to sleep upon the sands of one or another of the small beaches.

Skitwarroes and Nahanada were about to join them when Gilbert, once again his hearty self, said, "Stay the night with us as our guests, Nahanada and Skitwarroes. We are old friends. I shall be the guest of your people upon the shores yonder."

Nahanada could not leave his people. Skitwarroes reluctantly agreed to stay, together with another brave. The two settled upon their deerskin robes, but they were not to sleep deeply in spite of their feasting. Skitwarroes lay as if he knew a catamount with eyes like coals of fire in the darkness waited on a branch to spring on him. He did not trust these English more.

He drew his first free breath only when the canoe flotilla had swept out of the river and put an island at the river's mouth between them and Gilbert's men. He was resolved that whoever of the Pemaquids served as guides to Bashaba for the English, he would not be among them.

They waited for Gilbert all the next day at their village. His sail did not appear. Perhaps it was the wind that blew so strongly the entire day which kept him away. Early the next morning a runner from Sasanoa came into the village. The Pemaquid warriors were to go to the overlord at once; the Tarrantines were coming. As quickly as possible the village was on the move. If Gilbert came later, they never knew of it.

Although that winter was long and bitter, the Tarrantines did not hibernate like bears. They kept the coast tribes on the alert as they traveled swiftly on their snowshoes over the hard, glistening drifts, striking here and there in raids.

When Skitwarroes next saw the English fort at the mouth of the Kennebec, it was deserted. No cannon poked their muzzles through the now-leaning walls. And inside the stockade one large building had lost its roof of rushes, another was merely a mass of criss-crossed and charred timbers. In one corner of the enclosure was a white wooden cross of the sort Skitwarroes had seen in England in the places where the dead were planted like seeds.

He poked among the ruins hoping to find something of value, but others had been ahead of him. He uncovered only a few nails and a cracked iron kettle. The gulls wheeled overhead with laughter as rusty as the ironware and a black crow cawed to scold the lone Indian for trespassing.

Later, one of Sasanoa's people told him that the fat old man had died during the winter and that all the rest, even Loud Mouth (whom Skitwarroes took to be Gilbert), had gone across the water in the early summer.

With them had sailed a part of the Kennebec forest. The English had built a ship of native oak. Skitwarroes saw the logs that had cradled it and the chips that had been hewn from its timbers. Both were turning silvery gray in the sand.

Skitwarroes gave the English scarcely a thought after that. The intertribal warfare increased until whole tribes, such as the Wawenocks, were wiped out. Bashaba was killed by a French musket fired by Tarrantine hands and his whole family was slaughtered. Sasanoa stepped up and took his place among the tribes. He became the great overlord for the whole coast region.

The times were troubled, but at least for Nahanada and Skitwarroes their kidnapping had become no more than a nightmare dreamed long ago. Now the danger of death was constant. Death waited for them behind every tree or rock that could hide an ambushed enemy. But it would be an honorable Indian death—to die as a warrior and not to rot away in captivity as might well have been their fate.

CHAPTER TWELVE

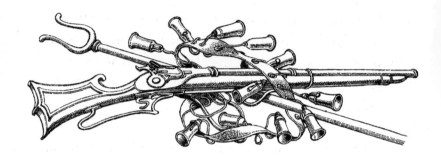

WHEN ASSOCOMOIT ended his difficult journey from Spanish slavery to Sir Ferdinando's home in England, he discovered what had happened during his absence. That Skitwarroes had sailed with a colony. That this settlement had failed. That Gorges, although he ought to have been discouraged about English affairs in the New World, wasn't. He was, in fact, glad to have the Indian return. He could use him for guiding another expedition.

By 1613 this new enterprise was in the planning stage. Sir Ferdinando had invited one Captain Harley to come to Plymouth and talk over his experiences in North Virginia, where he had been a member of the Popham colony.

Gorges was not surprised to see Captain Harley on his doorstep that day in 1613, since he had come by appointment. However, Harley's companion was a surprise to him, if an Indian at the door could be strange to that household which had already seen a good many.

The unexpected guest was Epenow, a very tall brave. He spoke a tongue which Assocomoit, who was summoned at once, could not understand. Gorges had to send off for the servant who had taught his three Indians when Waymouth first brought them in 1605. With his help, and because the two languages that the Indians spoke were not too unlike, the two savages were soon talking together.

Epenow told Assocomoit how he had been carried off by a Captain Edward Harlow (not the Captain Harley who had brought him to Plymouth). He had been sold two years ago to be "shown for a wonder" in the London streets. But, after a time, he "grew out of the people's wonder." No one wanted to pay a penny to see an Indian any more, not even though he was big enough to be called a giant. His owner was finding it difficult to get enough money to feed the strapping brave and keep him in tobacco.

Day after day Epenow's master stood outside the poor tavern on Fleet Street where they lodged. He called out, "Come see, come see the wild man but lately come from North Virginia, the greatest chance of a lifetime! Come see him as Nature molded him, all in his native garb, for a penny only."

Fleet Street in those days was the haunt of the wonders of the world. All around Epenow's barker, customers were paying out their pennies to see a two-headed calf, a mermaid caught in a fisherman's net, "now unfortunately quite dead," or a pickled sea serpent. Very few paid to see the giant wild man.

Then one day Captain Harley passed down Fleet Street. He had wild men on his mind that day, because he was soon to leave for his visit to Sir Ferdinando. It is not surprising that he paid his penny to see Epenow and, a short while after, paid a much larger sum to become the Indian's new owner. He had discovered that he came from North Virginia. Together master and man traveled to Plymouth.

All this Epenow told Assocomoit as soon as they could talk together. There was one thing that he did not tell him: his scheme for getting home. He kept this a secret because Assocomoit was to be part of it.

From the very first Epenow had noticed how the

eyes of Englishmen lit up when they talked of gold. They would look at his copper earrings and bracelets, ask where they came from, and then go at once to another question: Did he know the location of gold mines?

Epenow did not, but he decided to pretend there were fine gold mines at Capawick, the island where he lived and which the English called Martha's Vineyard. First, he told this to Assocomoit. He had sized him up as gentle and gullible. He would be so taken in by Epenow's talk of the Capawick mines that he would really believe in them. Then, when Sir Ferdinando questioned him about Capawick, he would volunteer that it had fine gold mines. The next step would be for Epenow to be asked to lead a party to this source of fortune.

It happened exactly as Epenow planned. The wily Indian knew his Englishmen.

In June, 1614, the gold hunters' vessel sailed from England for Capawick. Captain Harley, Epenow's owner, was aboard as advisor, and Captain Hobson was commander. There was also a party of English musketeers, the best marksmen who could be hired. Word had come that the Capawick Indians were fierce fighters and more ready than the tribes to the north to defend their lands.

Assocomoit was the most eager passenger aboard.

But his nine years of patient and painful waiting were to end with his goal almost in sight. Soon after he saw the shores of the New World, even before he could make his way to the Pemaquids, he took sick and died. Perhaps he was content after so much suffering and struggle to die in Indian country.

As for Epenow, this is not his story; he is not one of Waymouth's five Indians. But because the tale had a triumphant finish, it should be told. Very few stories of Indians' dealings with the white man have ended so successfully.

Epenow resolved that once he got to Capawick he would be his own man. He wasn't going to serve the English forever and a day, nor was he going through the pretense of looking for his imaginary mine. So he made another plan.

The English didn't trust him. They guarded him closely from the moment they came near the New England shores, because they knew that all Indians were strong swimmers. They dressed him in a long, loose nightshirt because they knew of Waymouth's difficulty in keeping a hold on naked, oily savages. All these restraints made Epenow more resolved than ever to escape.

When the gold hunters entered Capawick harbor, the natives came paddling out to them. The water was as dark with their canoes as if a flight of sea birds

had come down upon it. The Indians were welcomed
aboard the vessel to talk about trading. All the time
they stayed, Epenow was kept a prisoner in the
forecastle. His guards watched him as closely as the
cat does a mouse hole. But somehow, at some time
during the Indians' visit, he must have had a word
with his kinsmen.

The next morning the natives paddled out in
twenty canoes. The English, certain that they had
come to trade, allowed them to come near. Too near
for comfort, as it turned out. Instead of carrying
beaver pelts they had arrows at their bows, ready to
let fly. The oarsmen raised their paddles and held
them dripping and poised.

"Come aboard and welcome," Captain Hobson
called to them.

Not an Indian moved.

"Epenow!" the Captain shouted. "Come, come
here! Tell your friends in your own tongue to come
aboard."

Epenow bounded from the forecastle before his
surprised guards could get a firm hold on his nightshirt. He ran to the Captain's side and called out to
the motionless Capawicks.

"Come, come!" he called in English.

This must have been the signal which somehow
he had contrived to tell his friends to wait for.

Like a flash Epenow was over the side into the water. He surfaced and swam strongly for the nearest canoe. The flotilla moved in with gleaming paddles to cover his escape. The bowmen let fly a shower of arrows towards the ship.

The English were too surprised at first to make a move. Captain Hobson fell to the deck, wounded by an arrow. Several of his crew were hurt, too. Even the carefully chosen soldiers were caught unprepared, and ready was what a musketeer of those times had to be! He had to set his gun on the stand that was needed to support its weight, he had to uncover the powder pan, pour in a bit of fine-grained priming powder, cover it, and blow off any spilled powder. Then, *if* his match was already lit, he must knock off the ash and fasten it in the clamp that held it in place on his musket and blow upon it until it gleamed red. Then, and only then, could he squeeze his trigger and hope for more than a flash in the pan.

In spite of their surprise and the difficulties of firing, the musketeers managed to shoot at Epenow, and several claimed to have hit him. Certainly the Epenow who soon after was dragged limp and lifeless into one of the canoes appeared to the Englishmen to be dead.

In any case, they found it convenient to think that their guide was dead, for they weren't anxious to face the fierce Capawicks who were now so thoroughly aroused against them. They gave up and sailed away. Once more Gorges' hopes were overthrown. The wily Epenow had succeeded in his plan.

Nor did he have to die, after all, to accomplish this. He bobbed up again later in the accounts. No doubt from the deerskin mat where he lay recuperating he was able to enjoy his fellow warrior's reports of the English retreat.

And so Epenow lived to laugh another day while poor Assocomoit died as quietly as he had lived. For over a century there is no record of any of Epenow's people being killed by English newcomers. Perhaps that was his legacy to his people. His success, and the Capawick's reputation for fierceness, protected them, while their kinsmen on the mainland were being ruthlessly pushed from their lands and killed.

And now of the five Indians kidnapped by Captain Waymouth there remains only Tisquantum with his tale untold. How surprised he would be to know that his name is in so many of the books of early American history! Surprised and satisfied, too, for this humble Indian came to entertain great ambitions he would probably never have had if he had not been taken from his home by strange men from across the water.

CHAPTER THIRTEEN

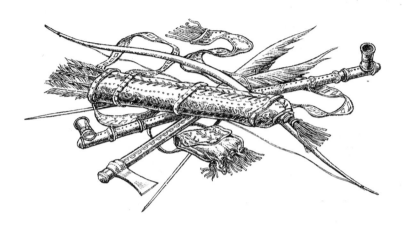

NOT A SCRAP OF writing has been found that tells us
what Tisquantum did in the years after 1605 when
he first went to live with Sir Ferdinando Gorges in
Plymouth. If he were used as a guide and pilot to an
expedition, no letter or report mentions it. When finally he does turn up again in the records, he is in
famous company. In the year 1614 he sailed with
Captain John Smith from England to North Virginia.

Captain Smith had left the colony at Jamestown,
Virginia, in 1609. He knew that he was saying
good-by to it forever. The handful of sad, loyal

friends who watched him leave felt that he might be saying farewell to the world forever, too. One night, not long before, the captain had slept in a pinnace moored to the shore. Somehow, either through carelessness or the treachery which was all around him, some gunpowder stored aboard the boat had exploded. Smith was so dreadfully burned that every movement of his body was agony for him. And he knew that unless he could get to an English doctor he could not live.

He survived the painful journey and recovered. London, perhaps, seemed to him a good place to end his years of adventure. Already, he had risked his skin so often and in so many corners of the globe that he had used up more lives than the nine proverbial ones of the cat.

But John Smith was a man of action. For him it was not enough to think about the advantages of American colonies nor to preach and write about them; he must do something active to further settlement in the New World. The Jamestown colony had been a bitter disappointment to him. He was sure its weakness was not his fault nor that of the new country itself. He knew that he had had the wrong sort of men to work with. Many of the Jamestown colonists were soft-handed men of fashion who had gone bankrupt in England and were completely useless as pioneers. Given an axe, none of them knew how to use it. The colony's leaders, too, were no better. For the most part they were men of rank or would-be gentlemen. They scorned Smith's practical ideas and deplored the thought of his governing them. To them, he was always the farmer's son and no more.

North Virginia, Captain Smith felt, might offer him more success as the leader of a colony. He talked, planned, and dreamed of a settlement there. In the course of time he found four London gentlemen who were willing to back a venture to North Virginia, both to make money and to acquaint themselves with the coast as a site for a colony.

He sailed with two vessels from the Downs in March of 1614. Smith commanded one, a Captain Thomas Hunt the other. And with Smith sailed Tisquantum as pilot and guide. After nine years he would see his native Patuxet soon. The little fleet sailed the northerly route and dropped anchor at Monhegan Island.

They found that several English vessels had already reached this narrow island harbor that was not much more than a passage between Monhegan and Manana Island, and were established there for a summer of fishing.

Tisquantum may well have been here before. Certainly this place was in plain sight of the Georges

Islands, where Waymouth had picked up his Indians. Long before any Europeans had come here to fish, the Indians had paddled out and used it as their fishing base. And now, for that matter, they came with their furs to trade. The rendezvous was a jolly, sociable place. The natives found good fellowship and plenty to quench a thirst.

The parent vessels where the fishing crews ate and slept while based at the island were like floating taverns, well stocked with barrels of "strong water." The men had brought musical instruments—zithers and giterns, oboes and trumpets—to play in their leisure. Here there was laughter and joking in which the Indian visitors joined.

Although the Indians always had a great sense of their own dignity and despised being made the butt of a joke, they had a strong love of humor of the forthright kind. Practical jokes and horseplay delighted them. Often on this lonely, offshore island their laughter and that of the hearty fishermen joined the raucous cries of the wheeling gulls.

So popular was Monhegan for fishing that every available piece of level, unwooded ground must have been covered with the staging on which the Englishmen dried their fish.

Each of these parent vessels sent out small boats to fish. The smaller craft were usually two-masted

shallops with a fore-and-aft rig. Four men were assigned to each—a master, a midshipman, a foremast
man, and a shoreman. The latter stayed behind on
dry land and tended to the curing of the catch. Soon
after the crew had caught the fish, they split them
and plunged them into brine. This salty liquid the
shoreman had to wash off before he could spread the
fish on breast-high staging, or hurdles, to dry in the
sun. He turned the drying fish as they cured and kept
an eye open for the weather. At the first drop of rain,
or when the gray fog curtain waiting along the sea-
ward horizon crept in, he had to get the fish under
cover lest they spoil.

It was among these fishermen that Captain John
Smith made his base in that summer of 1614. He
even planted a small garden that gave him lettuce
for "sallets" in July. His orders were to look for
mines and whales, for gold and whale oil were the
two commodities his backers most wanted. Perhaps he
had held these items out as sure bait for greedy
backers. Actually *he* believed in a surer cargo, one
of furs and fish. At any rate, the Captain went
through the motions of whaling. He reported that he
saw many whales and chased some, but they all
proved to be the wrong kind. What he did about
hunting for gold is not recorded.

Then he settled down to trade for furs and range

the coast. No doubt this is what he had intended to do from the first. He set most of his men to fishing, although it was late in the year for a good catch. He complained that he had been "lingering too long about the whale." Then he and Tisquantum and a crew of eight sailed along the coast.

They bartered for furs and collected information for a map of the region. Tisquantum acted as interpreter. Almost the first harbor they entered was the small one, now New Harbor, where Skitwarroes had taken Gilbert and his colonists ashore. Here they found other traders ahead of them. An English vessel lay at anchor and its officers were buying furs for Sir Francis Popham. From whom? From none other than Nahanada and some of the Pemaquids.

Smith's boat went on. Whenever they saw smoke rising from an Indian fishing encampment on an island or headland, or from a corn-raising village on a cove or creek, they made for it. They went ashore and visited with the people and slowly and steadily they gathered in furs.

More important, the Captain's knowledge of the country increased. To top it all, they were making valuable friendships among the tribes. Smith hoped to be offered even better furs when he came to trade the next year and to have staunch allies when his North Virginia colony could be started.

At the summer's end the patient Tisquantum asked leave to visit his own people. Smith gave him permission. He would pick him up the following summer when he returned from England. And what better ambassador of good will could he have than Tisquantum? The Indian could spend his time traveling about near Patuxet and on Cape Cod. He could speak with the natives for the next year's furs and spread word that the English were their true friends.

This partnership of Captain Smith and Tisquantum was a good one. Here was an Indian who enjoyed the company of the English, and an Englishman who respected and understood the natives. Not that he idealized them into faultless and noble savages; he had had too much experience with them at Jamestown for that. Unlike other English explorers of the time, however, he did see them as human beings to be admired for their virtues and not as a convenience to be used while they served, then thrown aside like a sucked orange.

It is easy to say now that if this strangely matched pair had had the colonizing of the New England coast in their hands, it might quickly have become a splendid development. "If only" is a game easier to play long after events have happened than while they are going on, as every one knows.

But the Captain was pleased with their partnership as he left his Indian at Patuxet and sailed for
Monhegan with the furs they had gathered together.
At the island he had them stowed aboard one of the
two vessels and set out for England. He had no gold
and information about gold and he had no whale oil
either, but he was not ashamed to face his employers
with his valuable cargo of fish and furs.

The other vessel was left with Captain Hunt, who
was to sail to Malaga in Spain as soon as the fish to
freight his ship had finished drying. The Spanish
city was a ready market for salt fish and cod-liver
oil.

It was a market for another commodity, too. Hunt
remembered this, and before he left New England
he did something that completely destroyed the good
will built up among the tribes by Captain Smith in
the course of the summer. It also endangered the
lives of any Europeans who might land thereafter on
Cape Cod or the shores of Massachusetts Bay. The
Pilgrims were to suffer from his act, as were many
who came before them.

No one has ever had a good word to say for
Captain Hunt. The men of his own time called him
base and vile. From all we can learn, he can't be
defended on any score.

CHAPTER FOURTEEN

AFTER CAPTAIN HUNT had loaded his cargo of fish and left Monhegan, he decided to add to it and make some personal profit. He cruised the New England coast and put in at several points on Cape Cod to barter for furs. At one of these, or it may have been at Patuxet, he came upon Tisquantum. For the Indian this meeting was a wonderful opportunity. Now he could show his tribesmen at first hand the marvels that the English possessed. Now they could see for themselves that the English guns, compasses, lanterns, and mirrors, all their everyday wonders, were not just figments of his imagination. Innocently he led more than twenty braves of the Nauset tribe aboard Captain Hunt's vessel. He wanted them to look about them and see for themselves that Tisquantum was neither a fool nor a fabricator, as several insisted.

Suddenly, here to Captain Hunt's hand, was a valuable human cargo. He knew that Malaga, like so many Mediterranean ports, had its slave market. It is not known whether Hunt had planned to capture a human cargo, or whether having Tisquantum's friends aboard his vessel suggested it to him. We do know that he ordered his sailors to close the hatches on his feasting, joking guests as they sat below in the galley. Then off he sailed with his Indian prisoners to sell them for his own profit.

Tisquantum's nine years' wait had brought him only a few weeks of freedom among his people. There were to be years of hardship ahead before he saw his native land once more.

It was onto a very different shore from their own green coast that he and the rest of Captain Thomas Hunt's shackled captives stumbled in the fall of 1614. Spain is a dry land, parched both by the hot sun and the wind blowing from Africa across the Mediterranean. The exposed ledges show like dry bones through its thin soil.

At Malaga, where they landed, Captain Hunt had no difficulty in selling his cargo of fish. It was his other cargo, with which he hoped to make his own fortune, that gave him trouble.

Some of his Nauset Indians went at once to the highest bidders in the slave market. Their fine, strong bodies made them look like valuable workers. Soon, however, there was a rumbling undercurrent of doubt running through the crowd that pressed about the auctioneer. Just who were these dark-skinned men, after all? These were not Moors who were offered for sale, that was plain, nor were they Negroes. Were they not Indians from the Americas?

By strict Spanish law these savages were not to be brought into the country at all. There was some head-shaking but, even so, the bidding continued while a pair of brown-robed friars pushed their way forward until they had the auctioneer's attention. Then they claimed the unsold Indians, Tisquantum among them, for their religious order. They would make Christians of them.

In those days the Mediterranean world was still one of slavery. Many of the large cities upon its shores had markets for the sale of human beings. In these the good friars spent their days, redeeming from slavery as many Christians as they could. For the slaves they could not free they tried to make their hard lot somewhat easier.

What the monks were able to do for Tisquantum and the Nausets whom they took under their protection we do not know. Nor have we a clue to the fate of the others already sold.

Of Tisquantum's life in Spain we know only that he eventually escaped. When next we meet him he is in London and knocking at the door of Master John Slany in Cornhill. He had been told by some seafarer that Slany's was the door in all England most likely to open for him into the New World.

CHAPTER FIFTEEN

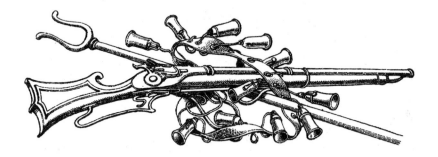

T<small>ISQUANTUM</small> <small>FOUND</small> <small>THAT</small> the seafarer who directed him to Master Slany was a true friend. Slany was a merchant, but he had much wider interests than the business of the warehouse over which he lived on Cornhill. He was treasurer of the Newfoundland Company, which had sent out a colony to that island in 1610. He promised Tisquantum passage on a Bristol fishing vessel crossing to Newfoundland in the spring. From there he ought to be able to make his way home. What was even kinder, the merchant took Tisquantum to live under his own roof until spring, when the two-hundred-vessel fleet was to leave Bristol.

Tisquantum was delighted to be given cast-off English clothes, a plain doublet and hose. A little snug in the shoulder, to be sure, and too dark for his tastes, but soon he found a purple sash lying in the muck of an alley and later a bit of tattered lace for his neck. With his dangling copper earrings, his copper bracelets, and his leather tobacco pouch he looked not too plain, he felt. He refused to crop his hair. He wore a red fillet about his forehead and a leather thong to club up his long black braid. He plucked the hairs from his chin as they grew. Let the Spanish and the English and anyone else muffle their faces in hair—he was still too much of an Indian for that. This was his appearance as he strode the dark streets and alleys of the closely packed city.

Now there was no need for fetters. Slany allowed him to roam freely. He knew that Tisquantum was too eager to return home to leave the man who had promised to help him. The Indian used the position of the sun to guide him about the city, or used as landmarks the numerous church steeples rising through the haze of coal smoke as he had used great oaks or pines at home.

Tisquantum, with his hatred for menial work, was

not very useful to Slany, but he could run a few errands for the family. Every shop or place of business had a pictorial signboard swinging outside its door, for not many Londoners were able to read a lettered one. When the Indian was sent to the "Peacock" or the "Swan" or the "Mermaid" not far away on Cheapside to fetch back a pint of ale, he could quickly find the tavern by the picture of its name creature on the sign. He could find the "Mermaid" quicker than he could leave it. Here there was music the livelong day. It was the foot-tapping sort that Pring's young man with the gitern had made for them at Patuxet. Tisquantum always stayed on to listen as long as he possibly could.

It was different when he had an errand at the "Cat and the Three Parrots." Slany sometimes sent him there with a slip of paper requesting some new book on American discoveries that was just off the press. Tisquantum hurried out of the bookshop as soon as he had the book. He felt slightly uncomfortable in that place where men stood with their faces close to the magic black marks on the pages.

His greatest trouble was in obeying the time god of the English, whose voice was the bell in a church tower, whose will was the sand trickling down in a glass. All his life until the kidnapping he had slept and eaten, hunted and traveled, according to his needs. He had slept when the sun disappeared and got up when it rose, eaten when hungry and hunted when the game was there. So in England he was constantly late for meals and the housewife gave up waiting for him. He ate when food was at hand and the cook would grudgingly dish up something.

This left him free to see all the sights. If there came a rumor of the King's being out that day, he hurried to see the monarch. Not that he admired him—King James was a small, tired man with a pasty face and spindly legs, and Tisquantum thought he would fare badly in a wrestling match with the Indian kings that he had seen. The King was always attended by a procession of people; this was the attraction for the Indian, this color and glitter of which the king was a part. Clothes of red and blue and yellow, silks and satins, hats nodding with plumes, steel helmets and breastplates like glare ice in the sun, steeds rubbed down till they shone like chestnuts fresh from the burr. To his savage's eye all they lacked was war paint to make the picture completely right. He walked with the King's procession as long as it lasted. With the music of flute and drum to pace his steps, he could have marched to the ends of the earth.

Sometimes the King's procession took place on the river. When he moved from one palace to another, from Whitehall or Greenwich or Hampton Court, it was along the Thames that he traveled. Whether they went up or down stream the royal party made a bright parade on the water. The King's barge, the Lord Mayor's, those of the London Companies of Merchants, were all decorated richly with carvings painted red and blue and gilded. Their long sweeps splashed in and out of the water as they glided past the palaces of the nobles on the river and under the bridge. This was London Bridge and it was like a street that had waded across the waters, carrying shops and houses upon its back.

Tisquantum always went to public executions, too. Like the multitudes of London, he felt their horrible fascination. The out-of-door ceremonies amazed him with their terrible barbarity. Prisoners, who had already been tortured, were burned at the stake or hung for awhile and then cut down, still alive, to be divided into quarters, or were dangled in chains over a slow fire for hours of suffering.

When things were dull on the Cornhill side of the Thames, Tisquantum crossed London Bridge to see a bear-baiting or a play in one of the theatres on the other bank.

At night he often crept out from Master Slany's when he heard the lively antics of apprentices. Although these young men had to work a long, hard day for their masters, they still had energy to burn at night. They stole out and joined whatever deviltry was afoot or made some of their own. Tisquantum could understand their wild, free ways, and when once he heard their singing and shouting, their scufflings with the night watch, he could not lie quiet on his straw pallet at Master Slany's.

Bristol, when he had said good-by to Master Slany and gone there to take ship, hummed with a different sort of activity from London's. To the Indian's ears it was a city of glad sounds, the work of ships' carpenters, of blacksmiths and riggers. They were making ready the fleet that was soon to sail westward like a flock of migrating birds to his side of the Atlantic.

CHAPTER SIXTEEN

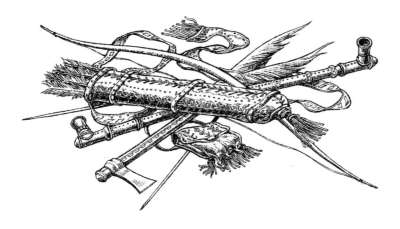

TISQUANTUM KNEW A GOOD deal about Newfoundland and the colony at Conception Bay which the
Newfoundland Company had sent out in 1610. He
knew almost as much as Master Slany did because
the merchant shared with him the letters he received, as Treasurer of the Company, from John Guy,
the colony's leader. Tisquantum knew that the win-
ters on that island were not as rough as had been
feared, that the humans fared well, and that their
livestock of hens and goats multiplied. He had even

been told of Peter Easton, the English pirate, who hovered off Newfoundland shores and was "troublesome to the English and terrible to the French."

The island, to the English fishermen who went there, was a good place. Its offshore waters teemed with fish and the small coves and harbors, like fingers on the hand of Conception Bay, teemed with fishermen. In fact, so crowded did these shores become that every spring the English vessels raced from their home ports to make sure of a place to set up their fishing stages on sociable Conception Bay.

After Tisquantum had arrived there and cooled his heels for a time, he found that it was a better place for fishermen than for Indians who wanted to find a vessel to take them to New England. He stayed on and on, still waiting like a player in the game of "Giant Steps" who had been told to take one large step and then no more. He could find no vessel to take him home. This waiting made Tisquantum as wily as Epenow, with his fictitious gold mines. When he met a Captain Dermer who not only knew Sir Ferdinando Gorges but was in his pay, the Indian saw his chance to get away from Newfoundland. Dermer was to meet another captain at Monhegan Island. Together they were to range the New England shore looking for the best possible site for a colony. Tisquantum decided then and there that the site would be Patuxet and that he himself would guide Dermer to it.

With this in mind, he described his native place as a paradise. Captain Dermer fell in with his plans and agreed that Patuxet was the one and only spot for Sir Ferdinando Gorges' colony. But getting there was not as quick and easy as the Indian had hoped. First they must backtrack across the Atlantic to get Sir Ferdinando's permission for Tisquantum to act as the Captain's guide. Then they would need more supplies. If Patuxet were as fine as Tisquantum described it, Captain Dermer wanted to have provisions for a longer stay than he first had planned.

With Sir Ferdinando's permission and extra supplies they finished the long, weary round trip and anchored at Monhegan in the early summer of 1619. By this time the other captain whom Captain Dermer had planned to meet had, not surprisingly, become tired of waiting and had sailed away.

Then Captain Dermer and Tisquantum set out on a voyage that both were certain would be as successful as that made by the Indian with Captain John Smith. They left their vessel and sailed in a pinnace, a small open-decked boat, with a few men. They were to gather in furs and knowledge of the coast on the way to Patuxet.

They soon found to their horror that this was to

be a very different voyage from Captain Smith's. At
the very first village where they called they made a
terrible discovery. Only a handful of weak, sore-
covered Indians were there. They had survived a
plague that had killed their kinsmen.

As the pinnace moved down the coast and visited
the ancient villages, the voyagers learned that the
same cruel hand had struck them all. Empty mat
houses were tumbling in, and the kettles, by tradi-
tion always kept seething over a fire, had long been
cold. Starving dogs skulked away into weeds and
brush that never before had grown so near a settlement.

Tisquantum's thoughts raced ahead to worry and
wonder about his Patuxet. But, in spite of his anxi-
eties, he patiently served as interpreter when Dermer
talked with the few Indians that they met.

Farther and farther south they moved. All was
waste and desolation. At Great Blue Hill they found
only a few hundred souls left of the Massachusetts
tribe. The year before this had been a powerful
people, able to muster more than a thousand warriors.

The sad survivors gave Tisquantum their expla-
nation of the disaster. It had been prophesied, they
said, by a Frenchman. He was one of three held
captive by the tribes along the Bay. A French ship

had unluckily been wrecked upon Cape Cod not long after Captain Hunt had sailed away with his kidnapped braves of the Nauset tribe. When the survivors of the wreck had stumbled ashore, the Nausets saw a chance for revenge. They murdered all but three after they had reached shore through the wild breakers. Those they let live, they passed along from tribe to tribe for whatever abuse the tribes could devise.

Now, even in this nightmare existence, one of the captives had managed to save a small black book (it was perhaps a Testament). When the poor man had a rare moment of peace he read it. By the time he had survived the Indians' mistreatment all along the Bay and had reached the Massachusetts, he read it with a dogged desperation which mystified the Indians. They suspected there was magic in the small black marks on the pages.

They asked the Frenchman if this were not so. He said that the book contained prophecies and one of them was a terrible end for the Indians who had so mistreated him and his two friends. The Massachusetts Indians laughed at his words then, but later, after their captive died and the plague had struck, they remembered them. They agreed that this plague was what he had prophesied.

Here, as at the other villages, the bodies of the

dead and dying were piled high. The newly stricken ran away at once in the hope that they could escape. But the plague had already touched them with its deadly fingers and they died where they first fell. All through the forests for miles their bodies were scattered.

Yes, surely, said the Massachusetts Indians, the Frenchman's prophecy had come true.

Tisquantum translated this story for Captain Dermer. Neither of them understood how disease is communicated. They didn't realize that it was not the Indians' treatment of the three white men but rather their welcome of others for their trading trifles and "strong waters" that had exposed them to the newcomers' diseases. Dermer did not recognize this sickness, but he knew that it was not smallpox, in spite of the sores it produced.

As they moved up the harbor toward Patuxet a few days later, Tisquantum strained his eyes toward his village for signs of life. But long before he stepped ashore from the pinnace he knew the terrible truth. His people had been exterminated! The weed-choked corn patches, the ice-cracked birch canoes along the stream's edge, and the whitening skeletons stretched among brambles and bindweed told the story.

Tisquantum, home to stay at last after thirteen

148

years, wandered among the desolation. Gone, all
were gone, family and friends and his own future.
The powah and the sagamore, the gentle squaws
·and the placid papooses, the laughing boys and the
soft-eyed girls. He felt that he had lived too long.

In a daze he wandered back to the pinnace. There
was nowhere else for him to go. He continued on along
the coast with Captain Dermer.

At the first place on the Cape where they found
any Indians alive, Dermer sent out messengers to
call two of the Cape sagamores to him. They came
and through them he was able to ransom two of the
captive shipwrecked Frenchmen.

With their ransomed captives, Dermer's pinnace
sailed out around the tip of the Cape where the sea
rolls in straight from Spain. They made for Capawick, or Martha's Vineyard. Captain Dermer had
instructions to dig for gold here. He set to work and
while he dug who should come to him but Epenow,
risen from what the English had thought was death!
The tall Indian slapped his great sides and roared
with laughter while he told Captain Dermer of his
escape and of how he had outwitted the large English party with their crack musketeers. The Captain
didn't realize it but he, too, was part of Epenow's
joke. The gold for which he was looking was the
fictitious mineral invented by Epenow. He had made

it so real to the English that they were still seeking it.

Soon Captain Dermer had to return to Monhegan. He sailed there and found the vessel which was to carry him home to England waiting, freighted already with fish. But the Captain had a bee in his bonnet. He had plenty of provisions and chose to let the vessel sail home without him. What was the mysterious project that kept him in the New World? Without doubt it was the mineral resembling gold which he had found on Capawick. He set out for Jamestown to winter in the milder climate of the Virginia colony.

Tisquantum planned to go with him, but as they drew near to the beaches of Patuxet he begged to be set ashore there. He had had a chance to think about his future since his tragic discovery that his people had been wiped out. He had decided that, lacking a tribe of his own now, he would cast in his lot with Massasoit, a neighboring sagamore.

Captain Dermer agreed to let him winter with his old friend. He promised to pick him up when he passed by in the spring.

But the two never met again. The Captain made the mistake of stopping at Capawick on his way south. Again Epenow received him, but with what a different welcome! Like Tisquantum, he too had done some thinking in the past few weeks. His thoughts made him suspicious of the Captain. If he were working for Sir Ferdinando Gorges, it was more than likely that he had been given instructions to seize Epenow and carry him again to England. That was why the Captain hung about the island, Epenow reasoned.

However, when the Captain asked for a meeting to trade with the Capawick Indians, Epenow named the time and place for it. When Captain Dermer and his men went ashore to keep the appointment, they met with an ambush. Arrows and knives killed all but Dermer, although he had fourteen wounds. The Captain was made of stout stuff. In spite of his weakness from loss of blood, he got into the ship's boat and rowed out to the pinnace, where he had left one man on guard. This man dragged him over the side of the pinnace just as the Indians swarmed into it from a canoe. He fought them off and sailed the wounded Dermer to Virginia. The Captain died of his injuries, but not before he had sent off a report to Gorges in which he recommended Patuxet as the place above all for a colony. He hinted, too, that he had found gold on an island.

Tisquantum waited in vain for Dermer's return, not knowing what an important part he himself was soon to play in the story of English colonization.

CHAPTER SEVENTEEN

ALL THROUGH THE spring and summer of 1620 Tisquantum watched and waited for Captain Dermer. He took frequent trips from Sowams, Massasoit's village, to the shore in the hope of seeing his captain's sail. He questioned every traveler who came to Sowams, but none had seen the white wings of an English ship nor a bearded Englishman who inquired for Tisquantum.

By fall he had lost hope of seeing Captain Dermer. He resigned himself unhappily to staying on forever with the Wampanoags. With Massasoit's tribe he was neither hay nor grass—neither one of the sagamore's people nor yet an Englishman. Then, Massasoit did not make him one of his chief councilors, as he had expected. After all, did he not know more of the world than any of the Wampanoags? Had he not crossed the wide waters six times and seen other lands? But, in spite of this, Massasoit preferred to listen to someone else. This was a bitter pill for Tisquantum to swallow, even if his rival were Hobomok, the pinese.

To be sure, a pinese was a man of exalted rank among the tribes. He had to be of strong physique and rugged character. He was picked when quite young for this special training. Hobomok had passed successfully through the early years of trial and survived the later tests. He had eaten only the simplest foods. He had beaten himself with sticks and run through tearing brambles. He had drunk the bitter juice of herbs over and over until he vomited repeatedly. Then, in a weakened state, he had run out naked into intense cold.

Now Hobomok had become a sort of superhuman who feared neither man, the Devil, nor death. The

other Indians were sure he could not be killed in
battle. As for the Devil, the magic that Hobomok
could perform was proof of his dealings with him.

Even so, Tisquantum felt himself as good a man
as Hobomok. He was bitter that Massasoit did not
agree with him. He brooded unhappily during the
fall and winter until the day in the early spring of
1621 when he saw a strange sight. It was a sparkling
day. Every brook was alive with the gleaming backs
of herring swimming to spawn in the ponds where
they had been born. Suddenly Tisquantum saw the
high crown of an English hat moving between the
blossom-frosted shad-bush along the trail towards Sowams.

This was Captain Dermer, he thought. He looked
again, and as the hat came nearer he saw that although its wearer had English shoes and stockings
as well as a hat, his middle was unmistakably Indian. He wore nothing but a red cloth tied about
his waist. Here was not the man he hoped to see, but
perhaps it was one who brought news of Captain
Dermer. Full of hope, Tisquantum went to meet him.

Soon he saw that the newcomer was Samoset, a
sagamore who lived five days' journey toward the
rising sun from here. His home was near the Pemaquids, and Tisquantum knew him well.

In spite of their long friendship, Samoset refused to talk with him. He had gifts for Massasoit, English gifts of a finger ring and a bracelet and a sharp knife. He must deliver them before he could answer Tisquantum's questions.

Tisquantum had to cool his heels outside Massasoit's house while Samoset talked to the sagamore and Hobomok. His feelings were a mixture of hope that Dermer might be near and of hurt pride. Massasoit, he felt, should have called him in at once. He knew better than Samoset how to deal with the English, who must be not far away. The newly arrived sagamore had no knowledge of these people except that gained on his visits to the fishermen at Monhegan Island.

Tisquantum felt very hurt, but when Massasoit called for him he lost no time in going to him. As soon as the Wámpanoag sagamore allowed, he asked Samoset his questions.

"Is my friend, Captain Dermer, asking for me?" he asked.

"No," said Samoset. "There are two Captains, Captain Jones for the vessel and Captain Standish for the warriors, but no one asks for Tisquantum."

"Have these English come for furs or to fish?" asked Tisquantum.

"Not for furs nor to fish," said Samoset. "These are not like any others of the English. They call themselves Pilgrims. They have their squaws—" he stopped to show with his hands how wide and full were the skirts they wore—"they have their children with them. Already their houses grow towards the sky. They have come to stay."

When Tisquantum learned that the place where the Pilgrims had settled was Patuxet where his tribe had lived, he said, "Oh-ho." His heart warmed with pleasure. At Patuxet he might be more appreciated than he had been at Sowams.

The next morning most of the warriors of Sowams and many of the squaws followed the trail to Patuxet. The braves had painted their faces carefully. Some wore deerskin capes swinging from their shoulders. Tisquantum strode directly behind Massasoit.

When the sun was straight overhead, they reached a hilltop that looked across to where the English houses were rising. Here the party halted. Tisquantum went on as ambassador for Massasoit. It was not Hobomok, the pinese, nor Samoset, who had first seen these English, but Tisquantum who carried the sagamore's gifts!

With four braves behind him he marched proudly. He knew that all eyes were upon him. Down the slope, across the brook and up to the row of partly built houses they went. Samoset led them to the Governor of the Pilgrims.

"Welcome, Englishman," Samoset said. He spoke English as a child does and had to point a good deal for lack of words.

Soon Tisquantum stepped forward to let the Pilgrims know that here was an Indian who could speak their tongue well.

"I am Tisquantum, of this place, Patuxet," he said.

When the Governor, whose name was Carver, spoke seriously and kindly to him, his lonely, shrunken heart began to expand. "Now I am of some importance," he thought.

He told his life story to a circle of English listeners, and took his time about it. He enjoyed the attention of men of wisdom, as Governor Carver and another named Master Bradford seemed to be. They understood that if a sagamore could not call upon a Governor, neither could a Governor call upon a sagamore. Governor Carver chose a man named Winslow to visit Massasoit and invite him to Plymouth, the Pilgrims' name for Patuxet. He carried a tray of gifts—copper chains, biscuits, and butter—for the sagamore. And all this was proper.

Even before Winslow set out with Tisquantum,

the English were getting ready to receive Massasoit. Captain Standish, who was a little man like King James, only red of face, gave the orders. He sent the people flying about. Some he sent to the "Mayflower" to fetch cushions and a green rug, some to bring trumpets and drums and to don their best clothing. Tisquantum made up his mind, as he listened to the Captain, that Bradford of them all was his man. He would not care to dance while Standish barked orders.

But coming back with Massasoit, Tisquantum had to admit that the Captain had ordered things well. At the brook between the two hills stood the Captain with an honor guard of drummers, trumpeters, and musketeers. The gunners fired their pieces into the air. The hills echoed back the reports. The air was full of startled birds in flight. For a moment Tisquantum feared that there would be startled Indians fleeing as well, but only a few squaws upon the hilltop disappeared.

Then, to the music of the trumpet and the drum, Standish led Massasoit and his party to a partly finished house. At the open doorway Governor Carver stood, as dignified as if it were Whitehall Palace. He kissed Massasoit's hand. The sagamore kissed his, and they went inside to sit upon the cushions piled upon the green rug.

Now it was not Hobomok, the pinese, who was important but Tisquantum, the Patuxet! He was the tongue for both Massasoit and Carver as they talked together and made an agreement.

"Massasoit," he said in English, "will be the friend of the English. He will help them against their enemies and they, in turn, must help him against his, which even now are a tribe called the Narragansetts. If any of his people harm the English, they are to notify him. He will punish the offender."

Master Carver agreed to all this. When their solemn compact was made, the sagamore, still sitting upon the cushions, turned his white bone necklace until the tobacco pouch at the back reached the front. He took out tobacco, filled the bowl of his great pipe, and he and the Governor puffed upon it, turn and turn about.

After that it was like school let out. The Wampanoags in their red, yellow and criss-crossed black-on-white war paint took turns at giving the drums a roll and the trumpet a blow. The sound that came in ragged bursts from the horn was like the squawk of English barnyard fowl running from the axe. None could keep from laughing at the noise, least of all the blowers themselves.

Later, when Massasoit rejoined his party waiting upon the hilltop, Tisquantum and Samoset stayed behind. In fact, from that time on, Tisquantum never left the Plymouth people except to carry messages for them to Massasoit and elsewhere.

Although the English were wise in many ways and could work wonders, there was still much that Tisquantum could teach them which helped them to live in the New World.

He showed them how to tread out eels with their feet from the muddy brook bottom. He taught them how to plant corn in the warm weather when the elm leaves were the bigness of a squirrel's ear. He taught them how to catch alewives, members of the herring family, that ran up all the brooks near Patuxet to spawn in the spring of the year. He showed them how these fish could be used as fertilizer, planting them with the seed corn in a hill, rayed out like the spokes in a wheel. They must set a guard against the wolves at night, he cautioned, lest the animals dig up the fertilizing fish before they rotted. Also he told them how, if beans were planted among the corn hills, their vines could interlace among the corn stalks and use them for support.

He taught them all these "how's" so that they could keep alive, and many Indian "do's" and "don'ts" so they could understand the way the natives thought and thus live peaceably with them.

Samoset soon went back to his own people near

Pemaquid, but Tisquantum lived with Bradford as one of his family ever after. When he overheard a Pilgrim child say one day that perhaps Tisquantum had been sent by God to aid them, Tisquantum's heart swelled even more with pleasure than on the day he had first come to Plymouth.

CHAPTER EIGHTEEN

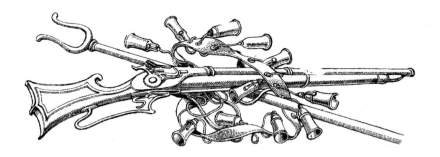

So, FOR A TIME, Tisquantum had the Pilgrims to him-self. He advised them at home and was their ambas-sador abroad. When six-year-old John Billington dis-appeared from Plymouth, he guided the party seek-ing the boy on Cape Cod.

Some time before this, John's brother Francis had had his turn at getting lost. He had climbed up into a tree to get his bearings and had seen in the distance the sparkle of blue water. "The sea, the sea!" he had cried out, but on going towards his sea he found that it was only a pond. It still bears the name Billington Sea. Perhaps there was not much enthusiasm among the men for stopping work to look for John when he, too, disappeared. Bad pennies always turn up, as Francis had. The Billingtons were a rough, surly family, held in contempt by the Pilgrims. Wolf talk and the worry of the boy's parents did not disturb the Plymouth men too much, although they did go through the motions of a search. They even sent off Tisquantum to tell the Indians at Sowams that one of their boys had wandered off and to be on the lookout for him.

Meanwhile they more or less gave him up for lost at home. Not even a tough young Billington could survive five days in the wilderness. Then word came from Massasoit that a white boy had been found by other tribesmen and taken to Cape Cod. At once the child became important. Here was an excuse, Tisquantum reminded the Pilgrims, to meet some of the Cape Indians and establish trade relations with them. This would be killing two birds with one stone. Tisquantum guided ten of the Plymouth men to the Cape.

As they crossed Massachusetts Bay in the shallop, they ran into bad weather. And they saw an awesome sight. It was a waterspout twirling across the surface of the Bay. This whirling cloud column.

filled with wind, sucked up sea spray as it came near. They watched it fearfully, expecting to be pulled into its vortex. It passed them by and they were thankful to be spared. Then they put in at Cummaquid.

Here they met the young sagamore, Iyanough. He told them that the missing boy was not with him but that he knew where he could be found. He offered to guide them to the Nausets, who were keeping him. He invited the Pilgrims to eat with his people. They did and several times told Tisquantum how courteous and gentle they found this Iyanough to be.

One happening disturbed the visit. While they were eating, an old squaw hobbled into the circle and stood staring at the guests. Then she burst into a fierce tirade, interrupted by stormy spells of weeping. Tisquantum explained the old woman's grievance to the Pilgrims. She had come there because she had heard that they were Englishmen. Captain Hunt, an Englishman, had carried away her three sons. She had come to reproach them for the evil deed and to get word of her sons.

Not even Tisquantum, who had been seized with her sons, could give her comfort. He knew that they had been taken to Spain. To ease her grief the visitors gave her presents. She hobbled away soon after.

Her story explained why the Nausets had attacked

the Pilgrims' scouting party the year before during the days when the "Mayflower" still lay at anchor off Provincetown and Patuxet had not yet been chosen as the site for the new settlement. The scouts had made camp at night and although they made a brush barricade and posted three sentinels, the Cape Indians had burst upon them. The Pilgrim guards had mistaken their cries in the distance for the howl of wolves. The savages made dreadful whoops that curdled the Pilgrims' blood as they came near. Then they let fly with their arrows but not a Pilgrim was hit or hurt as they drove them off with musket shot. They called this skirmish the "huggery" and until this meeting with the old squaw had been puzzled by the attack. Now they knew it to be revenge for Captain Hunt's kidnapping of the Nauset braves.

They left Iyanough and sailed on to find the Nausets. As soon as they landed where Tisquantum directed they were met with a hearty welcome, unlike that of last year. Tisquantum set out to look for Aspinet, the Nauset sagamore. Massasoit had said that he had the missing white boy. Late in the afternoon Tisquantum returned with Aspinet. A great train of the sagamore's people followed him all the way to the shallop, which stood in shallow water.

And there in the arms of a young brave wading

into the surf with the others was the missing boy!

He had a string of beads about his neck. His face was stained with the juice of the berries which had kept him alive for five days before the Nausets found him. He was blotched with insect bites and torn by briars. But he was well and happy, so happy with these new friends that at first neither Tisquantum nor the Plymouth men recognized him for a Billington. Never had he been so smiling, never the centre of so much kindly attention. He hung on to his Indian friend as if he would cling forever.

When the boy was home once more, the Governor, who was now Bradford, asked Tisquantum to guide two of the Pilgrims to Massasoit. Affairs at home were pretty well in order, he said, and now was the time to strengthen their bonds of friendship with the Wampanoags. Tisquantum agreed and on a blistering hot day in July he set out with Edward Winslow and Stephen Hopkins to carry presents to the sagamore at Sowams. As he strode along ahead, free of all clothing but his belt and his breech clout, he pitied the Englishmen wilting in their woolens.

They came upon a party of Indians who were at the shore for their annual lobster fishing and broke their trip by stopping with them. The fishermen shared their supper with them. It was corn bread and shad roe boiled with acorns. The two Pilgrims claimed the acorns to be too musty for their taste and ate little, which was a pity. It turned out that there was not much to eat at Sowams.

But Massasoit was not there when they arrived. They waited and when he came Winslow greeted him with a salute from their muskets which almost emptied the village of women. Then they presented the sagamore with a red horseman's cloak and a chain necklace. Massasoit put them on at once and admired himself for a bit. Then they fell to talking.

Soon even Tisquantum began to feel that Massasoit's speeches were overlong and tedious. On and on they went in this fashion:

"Am I not Massasoit? Is not such-and-such a village mine? Am I not the commander of their people? Why should they not bring their furs to you for trade?"

Since Massasoit held sway over thirty towns and each had to be mentioned in this way, it took a long time to get through the business at hand. Tisquantum saw that the two hungry Pilgrims were struggling to hide their yawns.

When the business was done, there was the tobacco to be smoked. Over his pipe Massasoit wondered aloud about the English king. He marveled that King James, whose wife had died, did not take another. Who was there to care for him if he had no squaw?

It grew late. Massasoit offered no supper. At last he did offer a bed. Winslow and Hopkins could not hide from Tisquantum their surprise at having to sleep with the sagamore and his wife. The two crawled onto the narrow mat-covered plank and lay down. Soon, even above the sound of the Wampanoags singing themselves to sleep, Tisquantum could hear the guests slapping at the droning mosquitoes, scrambling after lice and fleas, and sighing gently at the heat.

The two ambassadors rose rather stiff the next day to continue their official duties. These included watching games played for prizes of knives and skins. Later, Winslow and Hopkins offered to compete with their muskets against the Wampanoags' bows for similar stakes. Tisquantum laughed to see how quickly the offer was rejected. The salute to Massasoit fired yesterday was all the shooting they wanted at Sowams.

And still no food was produced. Tisquantum, who knew how often the English must eat, spoke to Massasoit. The sagamore went off with his bow and shot two fish called bream. They were good sized but when they were cooked and divided among forty people they furnished only a bite or two for each.

The second night was like the first in the stuffy hut. The two ambassadors were urged to stay on for more games. They refused because, as they told Tisquantum, if they were to get over the forty miles between Sowams and Patuxet, they must start at once. They were light-headed, they said, from hunger and lack of sleep. It was a comfort to have an old friend like Tisquantum to guide them home over the rough countryside.

The Indian swelled with a pride which he hoped could not be seen.

But as time went on, his old jealousy of Hobomok spoiled his new happiness. His rival at Sowams took to visiting Patuxet. Tisquantum disliked this and could not understand why he came. Was the pinese a spy for Massasoit? Was he the sagamore's eye, as Tisquantum was his tongue?

Whatever his reason for coming, Hobomok's visits affected Tisquantum in the sourest fashion. When finally Hobomok settled in at the Standish household as he himself had done at the Bradfords', Tisquantum's jealousy was overwhelming. He began to lie and scheme to rid Patuxet of his hated rival. After a time he found himself caught, as so many schemers are, in the net of his own falsehoods. Finally he became enmeshed in them until his life was in danger; it was luck, and luck alone, that saved him.

But before this had occurred one of his falsehoods had indirectly aided the Pilgrims. He had told it to impress the Wampanoags with the power of his friends the English. The Pilgrims, he said to them, had so much magic that they even controlled the death-bringing plague. They kept it, in fact, shut up in wooden kegs, and ready at any time to be unleashed against their enemies. Let Massasoit's people come to Plymouth and he would show them where the English kept the plague.

Now it happened one day that Tisquantum had a wonderful opportunity to do just that. The Pilgrims had at last been able to build themselves a fortified place, a flat-topped meeting house. They mounted their little cannon upon it, and under it they planned to store their powder kegs. Tisquantum was lucky enough to have Wampanoag friends standing by as the little barrels were being rolled into the cellar. He pointed to the dull black powder trickling from a leaky keg.

"That is the Englishmen's plague, as I have told you," he said. "They keep it there where you see so that at any time they can strike down their enemies with it."

The Wampanoags looked and fled in terror. They spread the news of the Pilgrims' great power far and wide. Word of it traveled among the tribes. That was why Captain Standish's return of a war challenge sent from the Narragansetts aroused so much terror in that tribe.

This is what happened.

One day a Narragansett arrived among the Pilgrims. He brought a mysterious present from his sagamore. The messenger inquired for Tisquantum but, oddly, was more pleased than sorry to find him away at the moment. He dropped his bundle and departed without waiting.

The Pilgrims picked it up and puzzled over it. Why should the Narragansett sagamore send them a rattlesnake skin stuffed with arrows? When Tisquantum came he was able to explain its meaning in one word—war! For a sagamore to send such a message, he told them, was the same as a declaration of war.

This was the worst news the Plymouth plantation could have had. The Narragansetts were a strong people, reported to be many thousands strong. The Pilgrims were in a weak state. Their ranks had been greatly thinned by the sickness that had come on during the winter. Their town was not yet protected by a stockade.

Even so, their captain, Myles Standish, knew the answer to send as soon as Tisquantum had explained the challenge: they must return one as warlike. He replaced the arrows in the skin with shot and gun-powder and sent off the bundle by Indian messenger. Later the Pilgrims learned that their answer had had a terrifying effect. When it reached the Narragansett sagamore, he refused to touch or even have it near him. He asked the Indian bearer to carry it away at once but the messenger, terrified by the reception of his burden, refused. Another Indian picked it up and started toward Plymouth with the snakeskin but after a time, he, too, caught the fear and laid it down. Eventually, after many hands had taken it a part of the distance and abandoned it, the snakeskin got back to Plymouth with all its contents intact.

When Tisquantum's lie about the Pilgrims' pos-sessing the plague was discovered, they knew why their challenge with its gunpowder stuffing was so feared. And they realized that the Indian's falsehood had no doubt saved them from a Narragansett at-tack.

But his next bit of scheming nearly lost them their firm ally, Massasoit.

A day came when Captain Standish and many of the Plymouth men had planned to visit the Mas-sachusetts tribe, near Great Blue Hill. They were going to barter for furs. As the sun rose out of the sea, most of the plantation families were already up and breakfasting. Suddenly a knock came on Governor

Bradford's door. Captain Standish stalked into the room, his face ruddy with anger. Hobomok came at his heels.

Standish pointed to Tisquantum at table with the family.

"Sir," he said to Bradford, "you harbor beneath your roof one of the enemies of Plymouth Plantation!"

"How so?" asked Bradford, rising.

"My Indian, Hobomok, tells me of an attack upon our settlement planned by the Massachusetts. The Narragansetts are to join with them. They have been awaiting such a time as this day when most of our able-bodied men are to be away. And *your* Indian, so he tells me, is one of the plot."

Tisquantum rose and crossed his arms over his chest. "If anyone is to be feared by the men of Plymouth, Hobomok is the man," he said, pointing to the pinese. More than this he refused to say.

The Plymouth leaders were in a quandary. They badly needed furs to make up a cargo for England, where they had left many debts, and they could not afford to lose the Massachusetts' trade. They decided to run the risk of attack and keep their appointment with the fur traders.

Standish instructed the men who were to remain at home to fire three shots from the little cannon on the fort if any danger threatened. He took both Tisquantum and Hobomok with him lest they make trouble at home. The trading party boarded the shallop. Tisquantum glowered from his seat in the bow at Hobomok in the stern.

The shallop sailed across the harbor and out around the Gurnet at its mouth before they heard a shot. A second one followed, and a third. Three shots—this was the danger signal. In a panic Standish ordered the boat about. Every man aboard pictured a bloody massacre taking place at home as they narrowed the distance between them and the town landing.

Once in the creek, the men leaped into the shallow water and waded ashore. They soon found that their people were safe enough but in a state of alarm. An Indian with his face torn and bleeding had come running into town. The Narragansetts were on the warpath! he cried out as he came on; Massasoit had joined them!

This was the worst of news. All that night and the next day the men kept strict watch. Even surly John Billington, the father of the lost boy, for once carried out his military duties without cursing. No one except the very young shut their eyes, and their parents looked at them fondly, as if they were seeing them for perhaps the last time. When Tisquantum spoke, Captain Standish now listened with respect.

But nothing happened. No enemy came. The elders began to believe Hobomok. He had scoffed from the first. Wasn't the Indian who came running in with the bad news one of Tisquantum's good friends? His wounds could have been self-inflicted. This was all a ruse to put Massasoit in the bad graces of the Pilgrims. No doubt Tisquantum wanted to rule in the sagamore's place.

Hobomok offered to send off his wife on an errand to Sowams. She could find out what was happening there and learn what was on Massasoit's mind. Bradford agreed to this, and the squaw set out. When she came to Sowams, it was so unwarlike that it surprised her. She told Massasoit of what Tisquantum had accused him.

This made the sagamore extremely angry. He felt that not only was Tisquantum false to him but that Governor Bradford should have had more trust in him than to believe these accusations. Massasoit sent off a messenger to Governor Bradford, saying that he himself was still abiding by the treaty that he and the men of Plymouth had made; whenever he proposed to change, he would notify them.

As soon as the reassuring word came that Massasoit

was not at odds with them, the Standish party set out at once for their trading with the Massachusetts. They soon returned to Plymouth with a cargo of furs.

A fuming Massasoit sat waiting for them. "I have come for the head of the false Tisquantum," he said. "You must surrender him at once."

"We can not do that," said the Governor. "Without Tisquantum how could the Wampanoags and the people of Plymouth carry on their affairs together?"

"Did we not agree when we talked at our first meeting that if any one of our men offended the other, to turn over the guilty one to those who had suffered?"

Governor Bradford had to concur; they had so agreed.

Tisquantum, translating his words for Massasoit, looked troubled. He had difficulty in translating those that followed, "And surely Tisquantum, in trying to create war between our two camps is an offender." The words almost stuck in his throat.

Massasoit nodded gravely.

"But," answered Governor Bradford, "much as he has offended, I can not give him up. He is too necessary as a messenger between us. True friends must have a tongue to speak for them."

Tisquantum was filled with a wild hope of being

saved as he spoke Bradford's message to the saga-
more. And he soon had the pleasure of watching
Massasoit, looking like a thunder cloud, set out for
Sowams.

He felt carefree only until the next day. Two messengers from Massasoit came running into the center
of the town. They were both in war paint; one carried
the finest of beaver pelts, the other a knife. To Governor Bradford they explained that the knife was to
be used in cutting off Tisquantum's head and the
pelts were to pay him for doing the deed.

"The English do not take pay for carrying out
justice," said Bradford.

Tisquantum stood by while the Governor talked
with the elders. They were beginning to feel that
Tisquantum must be given up if they were to stay
on good terms with Massasoit. Plymouth had more
need of allies than enemies.

Tisquantum threw himself on Bradford's mercy.

"If Governor Bradford decides that Tisquantum
must die, die he will," he said. He watched his
friend's face fill with pity as he withdrew into the
common house with his council to decide whether it
should be life or death for Tisquantum.

They soon emerged looking grave. Tisquantum
must die!

Before the executioners could carry out Massasoit's errand, a shout came from one of the men working in the corn field.

"A sail! A sail!" he cried. Others took it up. From all over the town the Pilgrims came, their work forgotten. "A sail!" they called out.

Bradford and his council looked out and saw a distant triangle of white moving across the mouth of the harbor. Here was a new problem for them. There had been rumors of hostile French along the coast. Could this be one of their vessels? It might be that they had come, by some agreement with an Indian tribe, to destroy Plymouth Plantation. The Governor and his men decided that nothing could be done about Tisquantum's execution until the identity of the ship was established. There might be worse villains about than Bradford's Indian.

Massasoit's messengers heard this decision and stalked off in anger.

The mysterious sail, as if it had appeared only to save Tisquantum's life, moved off and vanished. After a time, the watchers sighted it once more, tacking into the harbor. It was nothing more dangerous than an English pinnace carrying mail for the Pilgrims. It had come down the coast from the "Sparrow," a vessel sent out by Master Weston, one of the Plymouth colony's backers, to fish off Monhegan. Beside mail it carried, to the Pilgrims' dismay, a few colonists. To the "Mayflower" people these were only more mouths to feed from their rapidly dwindling supplies.

Among the letters that came was one from a complete stranger. He was someone who wished them well, the captain of a vessel fishing with the others of the English fleet. He had heard news of a terrible massacre in the Virginia colony. Three or four hundred English had been slaughtered there, he said. The Plymouth folk must be on their guard against the Indians.

This friendly letter was not only a timely warning to the Pilgrims; it suggested a way in which they could add to their supplies. The colonists were weakening with hunger. And here it was only May and it would be a long time before their gardens could yield a crop. Their food was almost gone. How could they feed the extra mouths the pinnace had brought? The "Sparrow's" men who had brought the newcomers spoke of thirty vessels that had recently arrived at Monhegan for the summer's fishing. The Pilgrims could picture the holds of these ships full of supplies—the bread and butter, the beer and salt meat, foods which they themselves had not seen for a long, long time.

Hunger made politicians of them. They sent off Edward Winslow to thank the kindly unknown captain for his warning letter. They hoped that he could be persuaded to sell them some supplies. Winslow sailed down the coast and found the captain to be as good-hearted on meeting as his letter had promised. He had not enough supplies to sell them any, he said, but he would *give* them what could be spared.

This kindness, of which they had met so little in England, sent a heartening glow through the colonists. It was almost as strengthening as the captain's bread which kept them alive, though barely, until the harvest.

As for Tisquantum's death sentence, it was not carried out. Massasoit never insisted on it and never sent another messenger with the death-dealing knife. Tisquantum lived on to be of further help to the colonists and less given to making jealous plots.

And the Indian was still badly needed at Plymouth. Before the summer ended Master Weston had dumped down upon the Pilgrims the members of another colony. They arrived without warning and, what was worse, without supplies. Because Weston had raised money for chartering the "Mayflower" and equipping its people, Bradford and his elders felt that they must take in the new arrivals. From the very first the newcomers did nothing but make trouble. They even stole and ate some of the precious seed corn needed for next year's planting. Eventually they did move off and settle in Wessagusset, in what is now Weymouth. The Pilgrims drew sighs of relief, but soon complaints came in from the Indians. The new colonists were stealing from them, too. In Governor Bradford's account of them, they were a shiftless lot.

But when the Wessagusset people appealed to him for help, he agreed to give it. They wanted the Plymouth people to join them in an expedition to the Cape Indians for corn and beans. The Governor permitted his colonists to go. Perhaps he felt that they could keep the Wessagusset settlers from rash mistakes. And, after all, if they turned the Cape Indians into enemies, Plymouth, being nearer, might suffer before Wessagusset. Bradford had not forgotten the Virginia massacre.

So the "Swan" of Wessagusset sailed to Plymouth and from there on towed the Plymouth shallop behind her. Bradford himself went along, with Tisquantum as his interpreter.

Across the Bay they sailed and out around the tip of the Cape. They skirted its outer shores, past the shoals with their breakers where the arm of the Cape bends its elbow. Tisquantum claimed that he could pilot them through these dangerous shoal waters. Hadn't he already been through them twice, once when he was with Master Dermer?

He may have, but certainly the conditions were different. The captain of the "Swan" had cold feet, in spite of Tisquantum's assurance. He refused to take his vessel through the shoals. Instead, he made for a harbor at Monomoy under the Indian's direction. The channel here was so narrow and crooked that the shallop was sent ahead. Her men sounded as they went with the lead and found it deep enough for the larger vessel to follow after.

Here at Monomoy they safely made harbor. Tisquantum turned at once from pilot to land guide. When the shore party came upon some Indians, he had to do a good deal of persuading before they would lead the English to their village. The bad effects of Captain Hunt's act were still being felt. Once among the houses of the settlement, they had to cajole its people into trading. They had nothing to barter, the Indians protested. Then some of the English stumbled upon a cache of foodstuffs that the natives had hidden. No doubt they needed it for themselves. Nevertheless, Tisquantum persuaded them to part with eight hogsheads of beans and corn in exchange for some English trading trifles.

This was the last service that Tisquantum could do for his beloved Bradford. He suddenly fell sick with what the Pilgrims called "Indian fever." He bled profusely from his nose, to the savages a sure sign of death. Tisquantum accepted it as such and there on the Cape, in late September of 1622, he made ready to die.

He told Governor Bradford that to him he left whatever he owned as "remembrances of his love," and that he hoped to go to the Englishman's Heaven.

How troubled the Indian must have been to leave the colonists before they were really prospering in the New World! What a bitter pill to swallow was the thought that he left his rival, Hobomok, behind to take his place with the English!

Then Tisquantum died and was buried on the Cape.

This ended the colonists' trading trip. They felt that without their Indian friend they could get no further with the hostile natives. They returned home.

There followed lean years for the Pilgrims, and the deepest disappointments. Beyond their need to make a living in this new country was the constantly pressing thought that they must send cargoes to England. There were debts for their first supplies to be paid. They sent back one vessel which they had laboriously loaded with clapboards and beaver skins. That was looted on the way by the crew of a French ship. Later, they sent off the "Little James" with a cargo of furs. That was run down by Barbary pirates. The pelts were sold at Sallé, a Moroccan pirate stronghold, and the crew was auctioned into slavery.

Gradually, however, in spite of these heartbreaking setbacks, the colony got on its feet. It was kept together by the dogged courage and supreme patience of its leaders, such men as Carver and Bradford and Winslow, and Standish, the peppery little soldier. When these names are spoken, one other should always be added to those who brought final success to the struggling colony.

It is that of Tisquantum, the Indian, and the last of his tribe. "Of whom they had a great loss," Governor Bradford wrote in his history of the colony, and he was a busy man with many problems and scarcely time enough to write words of praise.

AFTERWORD

ONCE THE PLYMOUTH colony was a going enterprise and other settlements had sprung up near it along the coast, there was no longer need to kidnap natives, as Captain Waymouth had done, for information about their country. The newcomers from the Old World could now get their facts at first hand. Using the coastal settlements as a springboard, they could travel on foot or trend into the interior by canoe along the network of New England streams. They could prospect for minerals, trap beavers and otters, and discover whatever medicinal roots the physicians of the day favored. They could cruise for stands of virgin timber.

Soon the debt owed the kidnapped Indians was forgotten, if indeed it was ever recognized. Tisquantum is the only one among them who has received acknowledgment of his aid. Yet, as one settlement after another was made by voyagers from England, each was made possible in part at least by the knowledge obtained from these captives, unwillingly and grudgingly though some of the information must have been given. Even Epenow, little as he would have liked to know it, aided his English enemies. When Captain John Smith set out in 1614 with Tisquantum, his backers had been inspired to send him by Sir Ferdinando's reports. And these were based on the information and misinformation he had gathered from Epenow and Assocomoit while they lived under his roof. There is no doubt that Captain Smith's backers wanted him to look for Epenow's imaginary gold mine! That John Smith had the wisdom to turn from that project to fishing and mapping the coast was fortunate for the Pilgrims. The Plymouth planters had the benefit of his maps and written accounts of New England.

The harder that life in England became as King

James' reign went on, the more widely read were the reports of returned voyagers from the New World. They were rushed through the presses and seized upon at once. They were read avidly, loaned to friends, and re-read. The Virginias were more and more in the front of Englishmen's thoughts. References to both bobbed up in stories and poems and plays. Actors in the London theaters spoke lines that mocked at men who rushed to the colonies and left their own and their countrymen's problems behind. Others praised those who felt that the new lands across the sea were the hope of the future.

Shakespeare, one of the playwrights, wrote his play "The Tempest" in 1611 after reading several of the travelers' accounts although, of course, not Captain Waymouth's. It is not surprising that he was interested in them. The Earl of Southampton was his great patron. He had long been a backer of American voyagers and it was he, among others, who sent out Captain Hobson in 1614. Perhaps Shakespeare was able to see the Captain before he sailed and meet the dark-skinned captives who went with him. And who were they? The wily Epenow! The gentle Assocomoit!

Conditions in England became so bad that the starving people from all over the kingdom came to

London looking for work. They dropped dead from hunger in the city streets. A third of that city's shops had to close for lack of paying customers.

Sir Walter Raleigh described conditions very well when he wrote of a time somewhat earlier, "Our prisons are pestered and filled up with able men to serve their country who for small robberies are hanged up in great numbers, even twenty at a clap." He added, "We should lead these people forth into temperate and fertile parts of America."

It is no wonder that the English swarmed out of their country when they were allowed to and had good men to lead them. Their desperate need for any sort of work that would put food in their children's mouths, as well as the desire for religious freedom about which we have always heard more, drove them relentlessly from home.

Their own plight blinded them to many things. Perhaps for this reason we can forgive their failure to see any good in the people they were displacing across the water. They saw nothing to admire in the savages' way of life. The colonizers were like a crowd that stampedes from a burning building at the cry of "Fire!" They trample down those in their way and walk over them, not noticing them except as obstacles.

At any rate, the pleasant days when the rock-

bound coast seems not to have been as unfriendly to
the colonists, nor as lonely as we imagine it to have
been, were soon over. Accounts of them are buried
in seldom-read books. Yet out of their pages will step,
for those who may look, the five Indians of Captain
Waymouth. A scene here, a word there in one account or another, and back they come—eager, inquir-
ing as monkeys, patient and gentle, loyal to their
fellows.

Tisquantum, Nahanada, Assocomoit, Maneday,
and Skitwarroes, whose kidnapping, said Sir Ferdinando Gorges, was a "means—of putting on foot and
giving life to all our plantations."

BIBLIOGRAPHY

Abbott, John S. *The History of Maine* Boston B. B. Russell Co. 1875
Arber, Edward, editor *The Story of the Pilgrim Fathers* London Ward and Downey Ltd. 1897
Arciniegas, Germán *Amerigo and the New World* New York Knopf 1955
Baxter, James P., editor *The Trelawney Papers* Portland, Maine Hoyt, Fogg and Donham 1884 Boston The Prince Society 1890
Belknap, Jeremy *American Biography* Boston Isaiah Thomas & Ebenezer Andrews 1794–1798
Besant, Walter *London in the Time of the Tudors* London Black 1904
Blake, William O. *The History of Slavery and the Slave Trade Ancient and Modern* Columbus, Ohio H. Miller 1860
Columbus, Ohio H. Miller 1860
Burrage, Henry S., editor *Gorges and the Grant of the Province of Maine* Portland, Maine (?) Printed for the State of Maine 1923
Bradford, William *Of Plimouth Plantation* Boston Wright and Potter 1898
Bradford, William and Winslow, Edward *Mourt's Relation or Journal of the Plantation of Plymouth* Boston Wiggin 1865
Culver, Henry B. and Grant, Gordon *Forty Famous Ships* New York Doubleday, Doran 1936
Dennis, A. L. P. *Captain Martin Pring; Last of the Elizabethan Seamen* Maine Historical Society Collection, Series Three, volumne 2 Portland, Maine Maine Historical Society 1904
Drake, Samuel G. *The Book of the Indians* New York Hurst and Co. 1880
Durant, John and Alice *Pictorial History of American Ships* New York A. S. Barnes 1953
Haring, G. H. *The Spanish Empire in America* New York Oxford 1947
Harrison, G. B. *A Jacobean Journal: Being a record of those things most talked of during the years 1603–1606* London Routledge 1941
Hosmer, J. K., editor *Original Narratives of Early American History* (Winthrop's *Journals*, volumes 1 and 2) New York Scribner's 1908
Howe, Henry F. *Prologue to New England* New York Farrar and Rinehart 1943
Jenness, John *The Isles of Shoals, an historic sketch* New York Hurd and Houghton 1873
Josselyn, John *An Account of Two Voyages to New England* London 1673 Reprinted Boston W. Veazie 1865
Kingsley, Charles *Westward Ho!* New York Scribner's 1920
McFarland, Raymond *A History of the New England Fisheries* Philadelphia University of Pennsylvania 1911
Philadelphia University of Pennsylvania 1911
Morison, Samuel Eliot *Builders of the Bay Colony* Boston Houghton Mifflin Co. 1936
Morton, Thomas *The New English Canaan* Amsterdam 1967 Prince Society Reprint Boston 1883
Moses, Bernard *Report on the Casa de "Contratación"* Washington American Historical Society 1895
Mundy, Peter *The Travels of Peter Mundy in Europe and Asia 1698–1667* Cambridge, England The Hakluyt Society 1907–1936

Notestein, Wallace *The English People on the Eve of Colonization*
New York Harper and Co. 1954
Purchas, Samuel *Hakluyt Posthumus or Purchas His Pilgrimes containing a
History of the World in Sea Voyages and Land Travels
by Englishmen and others* Glasgow J. Maclehose 1906–1907
Rhys, Ernest, editor *Chronicles of the Pilgrim Fathers* New York Dutton
Everyman's Library 1910
Rowse, A. L. *The Expansion of Elizabethan England* London St. Martin's
Press 1950
Robinson, Gregory *Ships That Have Made History* New York
Kennedy Bros. 1936
Rundall, Thomas *Narratives of Voyages Towards the Northwest* London
The Hakluyt Society 1849
Rye, William Brenchley *England As Seen by Elizabeth and James the First*
London Smith 1865
Sabine, Lorenzo *Report on the Principal Fisheries of the American Seas
Annual Report of the Secretary on State of the Finances* Washington
U.S. Treasury Dept. 1853
Shakespeare, William *The Tempest* London Dent (The New Temple
Shakespeare) 1935
Strachey, William *The History of Travel into Virginia Britannia* London
The Hakluyt Society 1849
Trevelyan, George M. *England Under the Stuarts* London Methuen 1930
Tunis, Edwin *Weapons; A Pictorial History* Cleveland, Ohio World 1954
Williamson, William D. *The History of the State of Maine* Hallowell,
Maine Glazier, Masters and Co. 1832
Willison, George F. *Saints and Strangers* New York Reynal and
Hitchcock 1945
Winship, George P., editor *Sailors' Narratives of Voyages Along the New
England Coast 1524–1624* Boston Houghton, Mifflin Co. 1905
Wood, William *Elizabethan Sea Dogs, a Chronicle of Drake and His
Companions* New Haven, Conn. Yale University Press 1918
Wood, William *New England's Prospects* London Thomas Cotes Corne-
hill 1634 [Boston (?) Reprinted for E. M. Boynton, 1898 (?)]
Villers Alan *Wild Ocean* New York McGraw-Hill 1957

INDEX